preface, p. 10
introduction, p. 17
geology of the M25, p. 26
historical notes, p. 28

J1a-J2

The Dartford River Crossing, p. 33

J2-J5

Over the Chalk, p. 59

J5-J7

Along the Escarpment, p. 89

J7-J9

Over the Chalk Again, p. 129

Gault clay exavated adjacent to Clacket Lane Services

J9-J12

Gravel, Sand and Two Rivers, p. 143

J12-J16

Gravel and Water, p. 169

J16-J22

Clay Hills and the Colne Valley, p. 197

J22-J26

On to the Lea, p. 227

J26-J31

Back to the Crossing, p. 265

places to see, p. 305
about the author, p. 309

index, p. 312

Evening falls on the M25

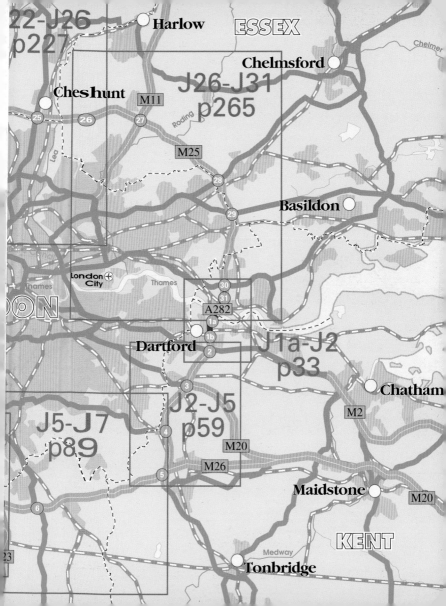

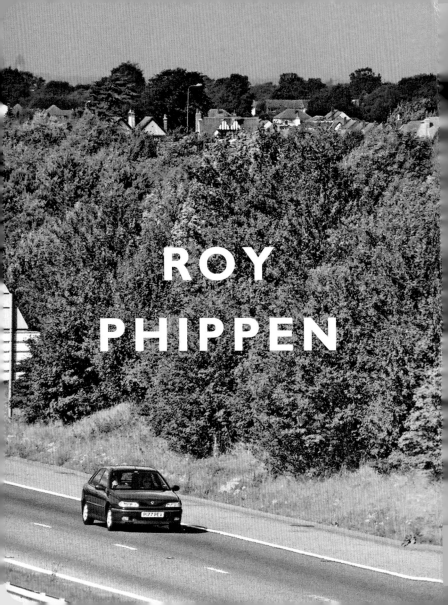

TRAVELLING

M25

CLOCKWISE

Preface

Preface

AS A CAB DRIVER working in the Sevenoaks district of Kent, it is my lot to travel almost daily around the M25 to Heathrow. Although the southern route is some eight miles shorter, conditions regularly compel us cabbies to use the northern section, making us familiar with both. All too often we travel one way empty, which provides the opportunity of leaving the motorway to satisfy our curiosity about places either side.

As my passengers are now totally fed up with being bombarded with information when all they want to do is reach the airport on

'Where's this bridge we're opening?' Trumpeters bound for the official opening of the River Crossing

time, I thought I should write it all down, get it out of my system and let them read it if they choose. It may just also be that this book might make your own journey more interesting.

Being a circular road, the M25 has no beginning, no end and does not go anywhere but back, eventually, where it was. In describing such a road some order has to be imposed. The authorities have helped by numbering the junctions from the Dartford Crossing and thereby providing a start and finish. However, numbers appeal little to the imagination, and to say 'The sun was rising over J23' would be ridiculous. I have therefore divided the M25 into nine sections based generally on the local geology, which is so distinct in the chalk of Kent though less so in the clays of Hertfordshire.

Then, sitting with voice recorder on dash-board, I have attempted a description of each section so that drivers unfamiliar with that part of the country may relate to it. These summary descriptions begin each chapter.

After the description comes some information about the construction of the section – it being so easy to cross the Wey Navigation (J10-J11) or even the Thames (J13) without realizing it or appreciating the effort which went into the bridging.

Finally a third part deals with historical and background information. These descriptions sprang from questions asked in the car by customers which led to my leaving the road to find answers. The result may fit in with J. Thorne's introduction to his *Environs of London* (1876), where he writes:

No pretence is made of exhaustive treatment; rather it is offered as a series of rapid though faithful sketches to serve for indication and suggestion. To ensure accuracy every place has been visited and most places several times.

And he did not have to take photographs!

Directions are given to some points of inter-est, and opening hours of sights marked with a ✿ are given at the back of the book.

As with all travellers on this most unreliable of roads, I wish you the best of luck.

RP
West Kingsdown, Winter 2004

The M25 – an introduction

THE M25 IS A CIRCULAR MOTORWAY, 117 miles in length. Although the concept of a ring road is now common and one can point to the **Périphérique** in Paris or the Ring round Rotterdam, this was not so a hundred years ago when a circular road round London was first suggested.

From idea to construction

In 1902, with the city's streets full of horse-drawn traffic, the London County Council was having trouble with what they termed 'cross-traffic' at junctions. It takes little imagination to envisage a scene where frustrated drivers of carts, hansom cabs and omnibuses, all armed with whips and within easy shouting distance of each other, jostled their way over cross roads. In 1902 the LCC resolved that:

Having regard to the fact that the traffic in main thoroughfares becomes daily more congested and that such congestion, though assisted by the

Previous page: Traffic flowing freely near J2
Opposite: Traffic jams at Fleet Street, c. 1880

mixture of slow and fast draught and the narrow-
ness of the streets, is even more certainly caused
by cross-traffic, it be an instruction to the
Improvement Committee to consider the possibili-
ties of some 'over and under' arrangement by
means of bridges or subways in or about every
spot where two large streams of vehicles have now
perforce to wait to cross each other.

**The Council's Chief Engineer duly wrote off
this idea by reporting that, 'Difficulties in connection with gradients, sewers and other
underground work' made it impossible,
although, of course, at a few sites one sees
later 'over and under' systems working today:
at the north end of Waterloo Bridge, in the
Euston Road and High Holborn (where the
Holborn Viaduct eliminated two steep gradients that were particularly difficult for horses).**

**Three years later, in 1905, a Royal
Commission proposed the building of an
orbital road round the capital at a radius of
twelve miles. I leave the reader to conjure up
a vision of this road of however many lanes, full**

of horses and waggons, supplied with water troughs and patrolled by wheelwrights and farriers to deal with breakdowns. In the event, the suggestion came to naught as traffic became swiftly motorised, traffic lights became common, and the Great War intervened.

Between the wars the government adopted a policy of 'arterial' roads, that is, improved main thoroughfares which allowed traffic to flow more easily to and from the heart of London. These were aided by 'cross routes' which gave access from one arterial to another without passing through the centre. A characteristic of such roads was the parade of shops with its own feeder road set back from the main highway so that parked cars caused no hindrance. There was also an 'inner circular road' that ran, as today, via the Tower, Kings Cross etc., and also a South Circular Road, although its northern counterpart was called a 'cross route'. A report of 1959 states:

Between the completion of Kingsway/Aldwych in 1905 and the outbreak of war in 1939 substantial roadworks in Central London were mainly concerned with the river crossings (six Thames bridges being re-built, one widened and the Rotherhithe Tunnel constructed), widening of main roads in connection with the tramway system, arterial roads mainly on the south-eastern outskirts, and part of the South Circular Road.

A census of 1948 identified only 15% of traffic as being through-traffic in the capital. It helped that London's main supplies were all delivered to the central docks and railway termini before being distributed, a situation that was generally assumed to be permanent.

In 1941-3 was published the Abercrombie Report which suggested that London be considered for planning purposes in four concentric bands and that each, lettered 'a' to 'd' be provided with its own circular road. Watford rejoiced at the thought of getting by-pass 'd' but one

The Abercrombie circular roads, with the M25 as built in red

suspects that the more fashionable areas shud-dered at the route of 'a':

A possible inner ring motorway about 11 miles in length with three traffic lanes in each direction for most of its length, mainly in the form of a sunken road on the north side of the Thames, in tunnel under Hyde Park and on viaduct south of the Thames and with nine access points. The line of the route was Eaton Square (Belgravia), The Angel (Islington), Gardiners Corner (Poplar), Abbey St (Bermondsey), Eaton Square.

The word 'motorway' has now appeared. Motorways already existed in America and Germany. Occasionally they were referred to as 'motor roads'. Their essential features are that they are for motor traffic only, that there is no stopping on them and that access to them is limited.

Meanwhile out in 'd' ring country around Watford, the road was not forgotten; it appeared in no fewer than nine different town and county planning reports between 1920 and

1970. Their road was to be a 'parkway' – one imagines broad verges, leafy trees and shrubs up the middle. In June 1939 the Evening Standard published a map of what they called 'The Great London Road' which followed the line of the southern section of the present M25, and would have connected the southern radial routes out of London. Of anything to the north there was no mention.

However, while the idea of the M25 was slowly forming, so was another and equally powerful one. Towards the end of the last century, alarmed by the spread of urban development, the LCC began to buy up green areas to render them 'safe' as they put it, 'from spoliation'. In 1878 the Open Spaces Act enabled the Corporation of London to acquire land within 25 miles of the City for 'the recreation and enjoyment of the public'. This growth in what we now term a 'green' policy climaxed in the legislation for a Green Belt around the capital in 1938. Inevitably the line of any orbital route would lie within this area. A clash was certain.

*An unexpected hazard:
dene hole appearing
near J5*

As plans for the motorway were sent out in the 1960's so were demands received for Public Enquiries. Thirty-nine were eventually held which involved 700 sitting days – almost exactly six days of Public Enquiry per mile of motorway.

Work started in earnest in 1975, with J23-J24,

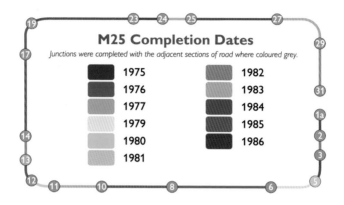

M25 Completion Dates

Junctions were completed with the adjacent sections of road where coloured grey.

■	1975	■	1982
■	1976	■	1983
■	1977	■	1984
■	1979	■	1985
■	1980	■	1986
■	1981		

and proceeded in a piecemeal fashion, as the public enquiries finished. Even during initial construction there was little idea of the M25 forming a circle. At most it was thought of in two parts like the north and south circulars. It was counsel for the Council (pardon me) at the Watford Enquiry who emphasised the local nature of the road:

The line of the North Orbital Road as approved was conceived in the 1920's and land was reserved for it in 1929 i.e. in the age of the model 'T' Ford and the Phantom... the line had been consistently re-approved over the years and had at all times been referred to as a by-pass for Watford and Rickmansworth.

On one Ordnance map an early section (A1 to A111) is marked M16 and another, close to Reigate, M25, where, obviously, it by-passes the A25. It was only in November 1975 that the Minister for Transport informed the House that:

The two roads would be subsumed into a single motorway ring – the London Orbital Motorway (M25).

Between this announcement and the original suggestion there had passed 70 years.

AT SOME TIME south-east England formed part of an ocean floor. By some violent movement of the earth's surface it was thrust out of the water, except for the valleys which continued to be washed by shallow seas. During this period, before the sea retreated altogether, sands and gravels were deposited on top of the other strata.

Geology of the M25

The M25, broadly speaking, passes through eight different geological areas on its journey round London, and these provide convenient chapter headings under which the motorway may be described. Travelling clockwise from Dartford they are:

J1 to J5 Chalk of the North Downs

J5 to J7 Hard sand and grey Gault clay extending from beneath the chalk which continues, cliff-like, just to the north

J7 to J9 A second crossing through the chalk of the North Downs

J9 to J13 Poor soil with sand and gravel interrupted by the silt of the rivers Mole and Wey

J13 to J15 Gravel amongst half a dozen rivers

J15 to J22 Clay soils over chalk buried deep beneath

J22 to J30 Clay with surface gravel

J30/31 An isolated outcrop of chalk forming the north bank of the Thames.

The main rivers are: Thames, Darenth, Mole, Wey, Thames (again), Wraysbury, Colne, Chess, Gade, Misbourne, Lea and Roding.

There are three canals: Wey, Grand Union, Lea Navigation; and three artificial rivers: Duke of Northumberland, New and Mardyke.

Walkers on the Wey Navigation, off J10-J11

IF GEOLOGY HAS SHAPED the motorway and influenced the plants which grow beside it,

Historical notes

man has managed the country-side as it appears today. Nine Roman roads cross the M25. Churches, parishes, parks and forests remain from Norman times. Wealthy Elizabethans built retreats among the clean dry hills and clear springs within a few hours ride of the City. Macaulay writes that William III could not stand London and its atmosphere, made up of

the air of Westminster, mingled with the fog of the river, which in Spring tides overflowed the courts of his palace, with the smoke of sea-coal from two hundred thousand chimneys and with the fumes of all the filth which was then suffered to accumulate in the streets.

And Earl Stanhope left London

to breathe a little at Chevening.

The M25 cuts through a dozen of these

country retreats, each with its own history.

Fifty years ago, travelling on this land, you would have been challenged by the estate's gamekeeper and very quickly ordered off. The motorway may have given you leave to pass, but its relationship with the land cannot be ignored, and a short history of the places through which the motorway passes is not irrelevant.

*The private chapel at Lullingstone Castle,
off J3*

The Dartford River Crossing

J1-2

ANY VEHICLE   AUTO TOLLS

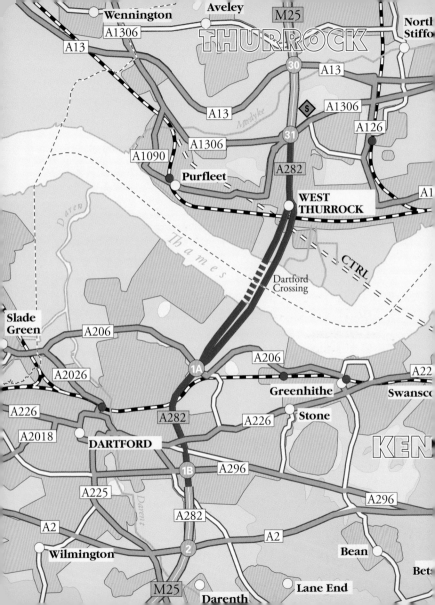

IT IS SURPRISING, as you approach the river from the north, to find the M25 in cuttings between deep grassy banks when for miles it has run along an embankment several feet above the flat Essex marsh. As the road rises towards the bridge what you will see will depend very much on which side of the M25 you are driving. The landscape on both sides is of chalk with enormous disused quarries cut into it. Each quarry is now crowded, as is the river bank, with industrial, retail or distribution units. The bridge affords a view much like that from an aeroplane during take-off or descent. The width of the river and amount of mud revealed vary of course with the tide. Facing the driver on the south bank is the power station whose chimney has been visible across the marshes for at least twelve miles, marking the position of the crossing when the bridge pylons are too slender to be seen. Prominent on the south bank eastside are hotels and a freight terminal.

Description
J1-J2

THE DARTFORD CROSSING CONSISTS OF

the Queen Elizabeth Bridge southbound and two tunnels northbound. Historically one has to deal with the tunnels first.

Construction
J1-J2

The older and more westerly of the tunnels originally had nothing to do with the motorway. It was built in 1963 to carry traffic in both directions between Kent and Essex to save drivers the long detour up to the Blackwall Tunnel or Woolwich Free Ferry. It cost the two County Councils £13 million, which they had little hope of recouping from tolls at that time. The tunnel and its approaches between the A13 and the A2 were designated the A282, which name has remained with it ever since. You may notice as you approach the crossing that the gantry signs above the road are at this point green rather than motorway blue. Not only was there two-way traffic in the single tunnel, but provision was made for cyclists: three London Transport buses had their lower decks transformed into cycle racks while two

The Dartford Tunnel Cycle Service being modelled by convincing cyclists, early 1960's

doors were cut at each end to give the riders access above. (To this day bicyclists are given special treatment: they get put on to a police Land Rover and taken across. For legal reasons a toll has to be charged, but it is nil.)

The second tunnel was finished in 1980 at a cost of £45 million, each tunnel then taking

traffic in one direction only. With motorway
traffic the tunnels became increasingly busy
and congestion at peak hours was inevitable.
A wait of one and a half hours was not unusual
and I well remember my car full of customers
who had landed at Stansted at 6.00 am and
were snoring merrily while I, at the end of a
night-shift, desperately moved coins from one
pocket to another in an effort to stay awake in
the queue.

The second tunnel, by the way, is distin-
guished by having green tiles in its Essex

Congestion on the approach road to the tunnel, as it appeared between 1963 and 1980

section, blue in Kent. The minimum speed limit – 10 mph inside the tunnels – is the only one on the motorway.

The problem of congestion was solved by the building of the Queen Elizabeth Bridge (which opened in 1995). The following facts might be useful in a trivia quiz or in keeping older children amused.

The bridge consists of three parts, a viaduct at each end and the bridge proper at the centre. The total length is 1.8 miles (2.9 km), the northern viaduct being 3,451 feet (1,052 m) on 21 concrete piers, the southern 3,307 feet (1,008 m) on 20 piers. Beneath the piers are 829 reinforced concrete piles driven to a depth of 82 feet (25 m). The bridge itself stands upon

four steel caissons or bins, each measuring 187 x 104 x 72 feet (57 x 32 x 22 m). These were constructed in Holland, towed 150 miles across the North Sea, flooded, sunk and filled with concrete so that they weighed 94,000 tons each. The bridge has a design life of 120 years, was built to withstand winds greater than

Painting the cables of the bridge

the great gale of 1987 and resist the impact of a ship of 72,000 tons travelling at 10 knots. Its height is 450 feet (137 m), its clear span 1,470 feet (450 m) and its central height above the river 213 feet (65 m). In its construction were

The unfinished bridge looking east

used 112 cables, 750,000 high strength bolts, 19,054 tonnes of structural steel and 48,000 gallons (220,000 litres) of paint. Inside each of the four concrete pylons is a two-man lift ascending to a small platform at the top, which makes the replacement of light bulbs somewhat easier than it might have been.

The building of the bridge was an early example of a successful private finance initiative. The commemorative plaque on the bridge crossing office states:

The Queen Elizabeth II Bridge marks the first time this century that the Government has entrusted to the private sector the financing, design, construction and management of a major road infrastructure project within the United Kingdom.

The project finance was planned and coordinated by Kleinwort Benson. The financing comprised loan stock placed with institutional investors by Cazenove & Co and a syndicated bank loan developed by Bank of America and provided by a group of major banks.

The agreement was that the shareholders would take over the complete crossing, bridge and both tunnels, call themselves Dartford River Crossing, and run the crossing until such time as the costs of building the bridge with interest had been repaid, when all would revert to public ownership. This occurred in April 2003. After a tendering process, the contract to run the crossing for the next three to five years was awarded to a consortium of three companies, Ringway, Babtie and Cofiroute. The name of the new company displayed outside their offices is 'Le Crossing'. And in case you are wondering where your pound might go –

All the proceeds from the charging scheme, after operation and maintenance costs, will be spent on transport schemes.

THE THAMES IS NO LONGER THE SLOW-
flowing river of mediaeval times nor it it any
longer as busy with ships as in
1900, when the pleasure gardens in Northfleet were said to
offer 'a marine panorama
unequalled in Europe'. We now
see only ships of modest size, mostly roll-on
roll-off, operating from a few deepwater berths
as here near the bridge. Cobelfreight operate
the one west of the bridge where you can see
hundreds of parked Vauxhalls and Mercedes

Gravesend in the 19th century

brought in from the Continent, and Rovers and Landrovers waiting to leave. On the south side of the river and east of the bridge is Thames Europort, operating a general freight terminal with ships running to Flushing, Zeebrugge and Bremerhaven. Oil tankers can be seen filling the tanks of the power station, the Esso refinery or the containers of Van Omeren. Another raw material delivered via the river is sand and aggregate scooped from the seabed, which goes to Civil and Marine.

The quarries on both sides are left-overs from the past. They provided lime for both agricultural and building use and later cement. In the making of the latter mud from the Medway was necessary. Similarly 11% chalk was added to 64% brickearth and 25% fuel in making the London stock brick. The fuel was found in the ash content of London's rubbish. By the end of the nineteenth century APCM (now Blue Circle) had no fewer than 280 barges on the river taking these constituents where

Overleaf: a Cobel freighter setting off down river from Dartford, the Crossing behind

they were needed and delivering their products to London and the south coast. London was building its sewers, houses, docks and railway arches; the south coast, its promenades and hotels. Barges could take materials via river and canal close to the site; they returned with mud or rubbish. The huge quarries were dug originally by men with picks hanging on ropes down the chalk face, their mates waiting with a trolley below — everything done on piecework. When the quarrymen got down to the watertable, the quarry was finished.

The quarries are now the sites of other industries. To the west on the north bank is the large building of Lafarge Aluminates, originally specialists in concrete for special purposes, quick-drying, sewer linings, etc., now an international ready-mix company. Next to them are Civil and Marine with their sea aggregates and then Van den Berg margarine. The red-brick factory in the distance manufactures packaging.

To the east, still on the north bank, are the vent towers of the tunnels, and two yellow towers storing Castle cement, which comes by sea from Lincolnshire. The grey storage tanks contain fuel and chemicals belonging to Van Omeren. The piles of containers are the stock, for sale or rent, of the dealers Eldapoint Ltd and Maintainer. After them come the roofs of the Lakeside shopping centre. Lastly in the distance is the huge pink building of the Procter

Procter and Gamble factory behind St Clement's

and **Gamble** detergent factory with its grey fully-automated warehouse behind it. In the shadow of this vast bulk, from which emanate whirrings and beepings, stands the small ancient church of **St Clement's**, which was restored at the expense of its enormous neighbour.

The most recent addition to the architec-

ture of the north bank has been the appearance of the **Channel Tunnel Rail Link** running along the bank west to east and threading its way unbelievably between the approach roads of

The Channel Tunnel Rail Link under construction

the tunnel and bridge – above one, below the other.

A striking feature of the **Dartford Crossing** is the number of hotels gathered on this spot. Calling at the **Hilton**, which is the largest,

I asked the lady at the desk why this was so. Her reply was comprehensive:

Our business is approximately 70//30 business and private. For business people this is a convenient place for people from the north to meet colleagues from the south, for continental peo-ple to come, or for people from the city. The M25 is a godsend – if you don't know the region you can find the M25; having found it, you must find the bridge and at the bridge you must find us. The Crossing is also an entry point to Kent. We have many tours stop here, tours, for example, of the castles of Kent. We also

Hotel at Thurrock Services, with view of Lakeside Shopping Centre in the distance

have at the weekends many leisure users amongst whom are regularly football teams travelling down here to play in London.

The most prominent building on the south bank is the power station. At 705 feet (215 m)

its chimney is 225 feet (78 m) higher than the bridge. It is operated by National Power, is oil-fired and produces 685 megawatts. Beneath the smaller chimney are three 35 megawatt gas turbines, similar to the engines of Concorde, which can be started in an instant. Before building could begin, the site had to be raised to a height of 50 feet above the river. This was done by using soil abstracted from an area just inland, thereby forming the lakes which can be clearly seen. Initially these lakes became a wildlife preserve, the builders donating their huts to the project and the local council providing a warden. Then came cutbacks, exit the warden, enter the vandals. It is now hoped a new University of Greenwich campus might incorporate and restore the site.

The building of the River Crossing and its approach roads did not entail the wholesale destruction of houses as had the Blackwall and Rotherhithe tunnels. The area was hardly prosperous; a local topographer wrote in 1861:

Lakeside Shopping Centre, with its lake

Grays Thurrock partakes of a picturesque and commercial character and is a town of some pretension. It stands at the mouth of a creek and had a pier 400 feet long at which many passenger steamers plying upon the Thames called and a regular communication was kept up with the opposite shore. The pier was built by a company in 1841 but the rivalry of the railway has drawn off its traffic and it is degraded to the purpose of a dung wharf.

That was in 1861. Four years later, Purfleet

belongs as the gatekeeper at the Botany will tell you, to the Government and Mr Whitbread and neither of 'em allows any houses to be built.

The 'Government' referred to the Royal Powder Magazines which were built c.1762 and stored 2,300 tons of gunpowder, packed in small barrels, in five sheds with walls 5 feet thick. The magazines supplied naval ships as they went downriver. Mr Whitbread was the wealthy brewer who built his house there, and it was his garden that was known as 'The Botany', a name which recurs at J24.

At different times old sailing vessels have been moored off both shores to be training ships for the Merchant Navy.

The low land beside the river has generally been put to anti-social use: Woolwich had the arsenal, Belvedere the sewage works, Dartford the fever hospitals. The north bank escaped with only the vast gasworks at Beckton, hastily removed by Parliament from its original site in Horseferry Road. The gigantic beam engines of the Crossness sewage works at Belvedere were too difficult to break up, so they survived long enough for the restorers to arrive❀, but nothing is left of 580 acres of gas works except some piles of waste known as the Beckton Alps.

Magnificent ironwork at the Belvedere Sewage Works

The authority of the River Crossing extends

well beyond the bridge and tunnels: it is marked by the 50 mph limit on the north side and the 60 mph limit on the south. In this latter section are J1a and J1b. J1b, at the top of the slope remains, as always, merely an access to Dartford and the A225, but J1a has recently been transformed. The development of the marshes into industrial units and the building of the Bluewater Shopping Centre nearby have made the junction much more important. Nowhere else on the M25 is there a junction labelled a and b. J9 is a double junction but is merely 9; J21 and J21A (note the capital) are different again. Enough of this nitpicking — on with the journey!

View back from J1b while it was under constuction: four lanes being added with the M25 in use. The slender bridge in the middle is a pedestrian crossing

Over the First
Chalk Hill

J2 to J5

IN CLASSIC NORTH DOWNS STYLE the road ascends gradually for eight miles to just beyond J4 and then dives down the cliff to J5. Between the river crossing and J2 the M25 climbs between brick and concrete walls on which are the outskirts of Dartford. At J2 the M25 passes over the A2(M2) which is itself on stilts above the Darenth Valley. A glimpse of the River Darenth may be had just after J2, before the motorway enters cuttings and embankments. There is then a long climb. Just before J3 westside is Parkwood Hall with tower and gables, beyond it the town of Swanley. Between J3 and J4 the M25 was designed to be hidden. There are occasional views of open fields west and glimpses of the Darenth Valley east. Just before J4 a road goes over to Park Gate House and a road sign warns of deer. After J4 the road descends quickly to J5. Half way down a pretty concrete bridge takes a bridleway over.

Description J2-J5

Previous pages: The M25 sets off – jam anti-clockwise after J1b

The beautiful bridge under construction between J4 and J5

The Tonbridge railway passes underneath and a rusting water tower marks the site of an encampment of mobile homes. At the foot of the hill, a stranger might assume that the continuation of the road in front of him is the M25. Not so! The M25 is to be followed via a slip road on the left. From this slip little is to be seen clockwise, but the slip anti-clockwise affords a view of Chevening village and estate.

WHEN THERE WERE ONLY two tunnels to be catered for at the crossing, the approach road to them with twelve toll booths was built in 1985-6 at a cost of £11 million. The final stage, for the bridge and 24 booths involved further widening and cost another £5 million. It was completed with the motorway in full use, an experience never to be forgotten by those who worked on the contract and unlikely to be repeated under current Health and Safety regulations. J2 to J3 was built in 1974-7 at a cost of £5.5 million including both three-level junctions. There was then a gap of almost ten years before the next section was built. During all this time, in the middle of the Swanley roundabout at J3, high in the air, unconnected at either end, stood the concrete bridge built to carry the M25, carrying nothing.

Construction
J2-J5

The delay was due to the strength of local opposition to the motorway. In fact the objectors pointed to the bridge as proof that, while

The Swanley roundabout with isolated bridge. The igloo (see below) stands where the surfacing materials are dumped, bottom middle of the picture

the authorities made a pretence of listening to them, they had decided already that the construction would go ahead. I suppose they were proved right.

The first and simplest siting of the M25 would have been through the Darenth Valley, used for transport between Dartford and Sevenoaks for at least two thousand years.

However this route would have violated an Area of Outstanding Natural Beauty. At the public enquiry, which lasted two years, nine alternative routes were considered, and the matter only ended in the High Court, in 1982.

The upshot was that the motorway was to run along the top of the hill, screened from view by embankments and unlit. It was then to descend steeply through the chalk to J5. This solution entailed a total 'muck-shift' as the trade call it, or excavation and resiting of 3.3 million cubic metres of chalk.

Muck shifting between J4 and J5

Used for this, at something like £200 per day per large yellow machine, were 27 scrapers, 130 rigid dump trucks and 50 articulated dump trucks for a period of two years. This section was the next to last completed in 1986.

THE MORE SOUTHERLY OF THE TWO

road bridges over the M25 between J1 and J2 carries the B2500, which was the

Background J2-J5

old Roman road known as Watling Street. This led in characteristically straight lines, still obvious on a map, from London to Canterbury and then on to the coast. On its way from London to Towcester Watling Street crosses the M25 once more, on its northern section at J22 near St Albans.

The A2, a relief road for Watling Street, crosses the M25 at J2, the Darenth interchange. Just to the east of here is the Bluewater Shopping Centre, the largest such in the country. It was built in an abandoned chalk quarry the size of Regent's Park in 1996-1998 by Lend Lease, an international property group based mainly in Australia. The architect was an American, Eric Kuhne, who was said to have been inspired by the 15th century bazaar in Isfahan in Iran, and who certainly did use the design of Kentish oast house roofs for the unusual wind chimneys that circulate fresh air into the centre. As 'an environment of retail excellence', Bluewater does not have customers but 'guests' – 27 million of them per annum – who are divided into Explorers (24% of the population, but 33% of Bluewater guests), Conformists (17%/28%), Discerners (8%/8%) and Traditionalists (18%/16%). Presumably the remainder come, like me, for the coffee.✿

Building Bluewater; overleaf, the finished product

The Darenth, seen just after J2, is the first of many streams that influence the route of the

The Darenth

motorway. Its sources are in springs in Westerham and behind Clacket Services. On its lower reaches it fed the paper works at Horton Kirby and, flowing through Dartford, made burial impossible near the church, the cemetery being up the hill or 'above the steeple' as a local rhyme puts it.

The large gabled building just before and west of J3 is Parkwood Hall, built a century ago as a convalescent home but now run by the Royal Borough of Kensington and Chelsea as a day and boarding school for children with special educational needs.

At J3 a large wooden 'igloo' has puzzled many drivers. It is in fact one of ten centres around the motorway used by the Highways Agency to store salt for use on winter surfaces. In order to keep the M25, M26 and M20 (which completes the triangle) free from ice, the igloo can hold 4,000 tons of rock salt

The Swanley igloo

mined in Cheshire. This strange building is a pre-fabricated wooden structure on 8-foot concrete walls, designed after an American idea: Buckminster Fuller's geodesic dome, which uses fewer materials, has a more even temperature and creates a natural airflow inside – all, presumably, necessary to keep the salt in useful condition. Swanley Maintenance Compound grits the section of the M25 between the bridge and Clackets.

The gritters are also indirectly responsible for the enigmatic signs that have recently appeared round the M25. They are about the usual size of road signs, are blue with yellow writing, and read typically 'M25, A, 38.3.' These are 'enhanced marker posts', which are spaced at 500 m intervals for the same purpose as the little white numbered posts every 100 m to identify where you are in case of trouble. However, these larger signs will mostly help the gritters in vile winter weather, who really do not wish to leave their cabs with a torch to find exactly where they are. The **A** signs are on the clockwise side, **B** anti; the numbers give you your distance from the Crossing in kilometres, very useful when most maps are still in miles.

The sign at Swanley

An enhanced marker post at 34.2

Motorcycles at Brands Hatch

Between J3 and J4 one may also find oneself surrounded by swarms of brilliantly coloured motorcycles on their way to Brands Hatch, only four miles east of the junction. ✿

TRAVELLERS UNFAMILIAR with this section of the M25 might be interested to explore the Darenth Valley. It contains four attractive villages:

Farningham

An old coaching centre where the London road intersected the Dartford-Tonbridge road. Its inns, mill house and High Street are largely unspoilt. Captain Bligh of the Bounty lived in the manor house. The Red Lion is a good spot and family-friendly, with ample car park and picnic tables beside the river.

Below: The Red Lion at Farningham Overleaf: the ford at Eynsford

Eynsford

Pictures of the bridge and ford appear widely on chocolate boxes and biscuit tins. A mile

Mosaic at Lullingstone

beyond the village is Lullingstone with a Roman villa of the late second century with bath house, central heating and mosaics. The site is roofed and admits visitors every day.❀ Beyond are Lullingstone Castle and deer park, which deserve a little more attention than a group of German visitors in my car were prepared to give it. 'Ein kleines schloss!' they said and that was it.

The first thing they missed was a deer park. Deer parks are a feature of the M25 north and south. Usually one, two or even three miles square, the parks were surrounded by a ditch and high fence to keep the deer in and dogs out. As the king had the monopoly of forest

The gatehouse, Lullingstone Castle

hunting, the rich applied to the crown for licences to build parks. Once granted, not only could they hunt on their own land but success was guaranteed by having the deer driven towards them in the confined space by the peasantry. Royalty also had its parks as at Theobalds (J25, p. 237) where James I had a ten-mile wall built round his. Characteristic of a deer park are its pollarded trees, that is, with their branches regularly cut back at a height beyond the deer's reach so that the wood can be used as timber and the shoots grow again. By this means the trunks of the trees, constantly re-invigorated, may reach a circumference of 16 feet or more.

The flat area before the gatehouse was the tiltyard of Henry VIII's time. Sir John Peche of Lullingstone was the king's champion at the joust, a sport in which Henry himself was known to break 17 lances in a day. Rabbits were also farmed here, in the area still known as 'the Warren', and doves in the huge Tudor dovecot provided a source of fertiliser and saltpetre for explosives. The castle and park have belonged to the same family since the 15th century, the family name changing from Peche to Hart and then Hart-Dyke only through the marriage of female members.

More recently there was a plan during the 1930's to build a commercial airport where the M25 now runs, and a housing estate in the park, both frustrated by vehement local opposition. Silk worms and a silk factory were introduced and robes produced for the coronation of 1936. Finally a fake airfield with wood and canvas

Eagle Heights

planes was built in WWII to take some of the heat from Biggin Hill. Barrage balloons were everywhere but a doodlebug hit the gatehouse. On the hill behind the Roman Villa is Eagle Heights, a centre for birds of prey.

View from Eagle Heights over the Darenth valley

Demonstration flights are held daily, but the centre is worth a visit for the view alone.✿

Shoreham

Another pretty village, though infested occasionally by Morris dancers. The painter Samuel Palmer made the village the centre of a

romantic movement about 1813. Tracking down his paintings proves singularly unrewarding, neither the Tate nor the V&A showing more than a couple of gloomy 10 inch canvasses. Michael Jacobs writes in his book on the art scene of England:

The countryside around Shoreham was Samuel Palmer's 'Valley of Vision'... His father was appointed Minister to the Baptist chapel at nearby Otford and set up home in Shoreham at Water House off Church Street on the banks of the Darenth (now marked with a plaque). Palmer moved in with his father and remained here until 1834. Water House became

Samuel Palmer: A Vision of Shoreham

the gathering point for a group of young artists including George Richmond and Edward Calvert... the long cloaks they wore and their odd behaviour gave rise to a good deal of local suspicion.

One wonders what Palmer Senior the minister made of all this!

The village cricket ground, approached by a footpath over the golf course, is a very special place. With the great white cross on the hill dominating the valley and with nothing more modern in view, it could be still 1918.

Otford

A village with several remarkable buildings but most notably the Archbishop's Palace. This, being almost on the same scale as Hampton Court, would have proved a formidable tourist attraction had more than the gatehouse survived. In fact Otford is just the first of many palaces around the M25 of which only traces remain. Others are, or rather were, at Bletchingley, Kings Langley and Enfield. Their disappearance should not cause surprise. With transport difficult, if not impossible, in former times, building materials were sourced in the

The Archbishop's Palace, Otford

most practical way possible. Many an English church has recycled Roman tiles in its quoins and arches to augment local supplies. Royal and archiepiscopal palaces were no exception in being sold off for their materials. Oatlands, built out of stones from Chertsey Abbey, was reused for the Wey Navigation canal (see p. 161).

Otford Palace was improved by Archbishop William Wareham, Lord Chancellor (at a cost of £30K) until he was replaced by Cardinal Wolsey in 1515. There was a rivalry between the two. Wolsey, from the comfort of Hampton, teased him about the palace being wet and unhealthy, and even Henry VIII described it as 'damp and rheumaticky.' In 1520 the King and Queen and retinue stayed at Otford en route to France and the Cloth of Gold. After Henry took over both palaces, Hampton Court in 1527 and Otford in 1537, Otford was allowed to fall into disrepair. Accounts from the demolition of St Augustine's Canterbury have survived to give one a taste of the time:

ii ode of flynt and rubyshe stone dygyd from ye mas hep and rubyshe of ye old stepyll and other places at vi d lood — xii d.
vi hard step stons - ii s vi d
iiii small round pyller marbull stons at vi d a piece.
ye olde leade

Otford Palace was eaten into and re-cycled. They might not have had Ford vans, but the gestures and expressions of those involved would have been very familiar.

To return to the motorway. After J4 the bridleway bridge which spans the deep cutting through the chalk should be noted. It is 60 feet high high and 250 across and as attractive as the concrete railway bridge near J12 is ugly. One can get to it by taking the old road from J4 via Badgers Mount towards Sevenoaks and walking behind the Polehill Arms. In summer spiders' webs fill each gap between the railings, making the whole bridge an insect trap.

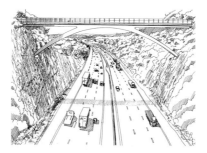

Along the
Escarpment
J5 to J7

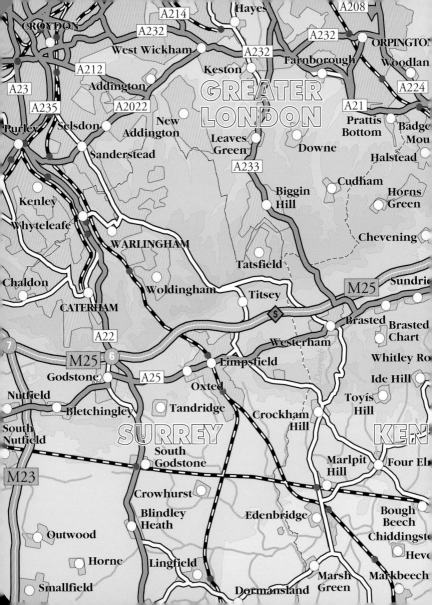

FOR REASONS TO BE EXPLAINED shortly, the M25 veers from its southward course, via a slip road, to head west. A narrow road passes over the slips. The M25 now runs almost straight and level along the foot of the chalk escarpment to the north. To the south views of Sevenoaks and the Weald are often obscured by plantations and embankments, while the view north is open. The M25 runs between many communities here: there are no fewer than ten roads passing over this stretch and four under. It is here, in by-passing the A25, that the motorway gets its name. Within half a mile southside is the first of many lagoons built to catch surface water polluted by the traffic and prevent it from entering local ground water. At 4 miles from the A25 a wooded area is bisected by the road and it is here that the service area has been built. At 5 miles one can catch sight of Titsey Place with its church to the north, and at 6 miles on the same side is the south lodge

Description J5-J7

Previous pages: excavating Gault Clay, near Clackets, to get at the sand beneath

to the estate. Thereafter a wooden fence
screens the village of Limpsfield to the south.
At 7½ miles there is a large chalk quarry north.
At 8 miles the London-Brighton railway issues
from a tunnel through the chalk to pass under.
At J6 a valley occupied by the A22 runs north-
south beneath the motorway. Just before this
intersection northside is a vineyard. A wooded
hill with brick water tower appears north after
J6 as does a large village, Bletchingley, on the
hillside south.

View from the water tower towards Gatwick, over the sand quarry at Bletchingley.
The airport runways are visible at the right

THE MOTORIST MAY BE SURPRISED TO find the main carriageway of the capital's orbital motorway become the A21 and the motorway itself become merely a slip road, but here he is experiencing but one of the great compromise solutions in the building of the M25.

Background
J5-J7

The town of Sevenoaks is pleasant, affluent and reputedly the home of many senior civil servants who enjoy its good train service to London. If the motorway had to be built near-by, Sevenoaks, they say, wanted to have the least to do with it. The M25 and M26 were, therefore, to meet away from the town at a point already occupied by the A21 and where the interdependent villages of Chipstead and Chevening would be severed from each other. The church and school were in Chevening, the bulk of the population in Chipstead. The Inspector's report following the Public Enquiry begins:

Not all of the 157 organisations or persons who objected, counter-objected or made representations have been individually mentioned.

Prominent were the Chevening WI, the Chipstead Evening WI and the head teacher of the Chevening C of E school. This was to be a typically English affair!

A census was taken of the journeys along the mile-long road between the villages. The numbers over a day were found to be:

Schools	22
Work	31
Shops and PO	98
Church Communion Service	22
Sunday school & choir practice	4
Recreation Ground	44
Sailing or fishing on lake	20
Scouts, Guides, Cubs and Brownies	2
Village inns	27

plus

Cyclists   2
Horseman   1

This local road could obviously not be abandoned. Various plans for joining it with the M25, M26 and the A21 were considered. My favourite has to be that for a roundabout. And that is how we got to the present compromise by which, apart from the silliness of the M25 becoming a slip road, there are two serious disadvantages. First, as a Sevenoaks lady who was arranging flowers in Chevening church told me — 'We can't get onto the M26'. Secondly the use of the M26 westwards is hazardous as there is no exit whatsoever for 18 miles between Wrotham and Oxted. Not infrequently the M25 is blocked clockwise and in the long queues formed on the M26 I have seen drivers sitting on the roofs of their cars sunbathing. However the inhabitants of Chipstead and Chevening were not forgotten. The M25 passes over the M26. The A21 passes over them both, and high above that is yet another long slender

bridge on which, if the time is right, you may even see two little girls on their way to Brownies.

Finally the two small bridges over the slips have to be explained. Three houses, one of them a kennels, were marooned by the construction on a wedge of land with no access to the east. The two small bridges use the wooded plantation as a stepping stone to get to them. As if these were not complications enough, a Saxon burial ground of some 200 graves was discovered and their contents reburied.

Saxon grave at J5

Having left the chalk the contractors now found quite different ground beneath them along the foot of the escarpment. The chalk cliff had been twisted upwards at some remote geological period and the layers beneath it exposed. These were greensand,

The solution: view from the Chevening/Chipstead footbridge over the A21, crossing the M25 at J5

a firm material, and **G**ault clay. **A** dark blue-grey in colour, **G**ault is soft and sticky when

Gault clay

wet, hard as rock when dry and at some point in between can crack open to reveal thin layers of rainbow-coloured fossils whose colour quickly fades on exposure to air. The engineers feared that embankments of this clay might collapse in the wet. In 2002 this stretch had to be renewed, possibly because of the clay.

Just after J6 the M25 has been widened to four lanes and a bituminised asphalt laid which not only reduces tyre noise but magically absorbs surface water. Travelling anti-clockwise at this point where four lanes reduced to three, just where the M23 fed into the M25, was problematic. Lorries moved into the centre lane to avoid cars appearing on the inside, and cars on the outside two lanes were left to sort themselves out in one. The extension of the

M23 slip road along to J6 has solved the problem.

J7 is the first free-flow junction on the M25. The M23 passes over for 1½ miles on five 180 foot (55 m) spans. Sandwiched between, two more bridges take traffic from one road to the other.

J7. The M23 runs S-N, top to the bottom, and the M25 runs E-W beneath.

BETWEEN J5 AND J6 the M25 crosses the estates of three men who were much more  than local figures. First there is Chevening a mile north of J5, then Squerryes a mile south of the M25 in the village of Westerham, and finally Titsey, screened by trees but just visible a half mile north of Clacket Services. The farmlands of these estates ran north-south so, it is said, that each parish would have an equal share of the poorer chalky soil of the hill and the better soil of the valley.

Chevening and General James Stanhope

Stanhope's father was English ambassador to Florence in 1688 and to the Hague in 1699. He put two of his sons in the army and two in the navy, as he thought this the way to advancement. One brother died of fever, two in action. James, by supplying his own men, complete with uniforms and horses etc., became a major in the Guards and fought in Italy, Flanders,

Portugal and Spain. He was also an MP during this period when campaigns were fought only during the summer months. Made commander-in-chief in Spain, Stanhope took Minorca and then, in a cavalry charge at Almenara, killed the opposing general in single combat, for which he received a gold medallion from the Queen. Under George I he became one of the two foreign secretaries and in 1716 Chancellor of the Exchequer and First Lord of the Treasury, the highest offices in the land. In 1712 he married Lucy Pitt. He was then 40, she 22. In 1717 he bought Chevening, planned vast improvements to the great house but left supervision of the building to his wife. When he died of a stroke in 1721 (while making a 'vehement' speech) he was buried at Chevening with a monument in Westminster. His wife died in 1723.

Subsequent generations enlarged the house and moved two ancient roads that lay too close for their liking. One was the ancient Pilgrim's

Overleaf: Chevening by Johannes Kip, 1719

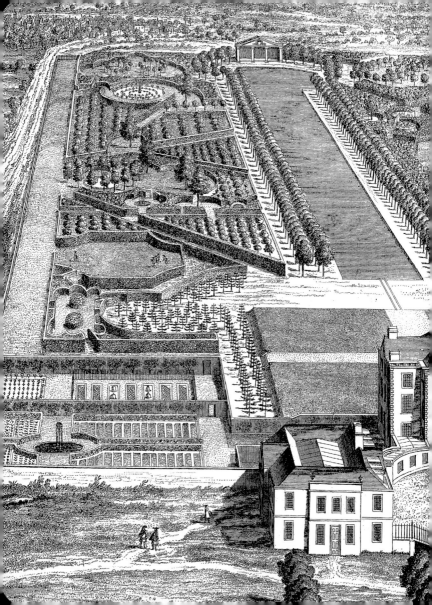

Way along the side of the hill; the other, the original A21 track used by fish merchants to bring salted fish from Hastings to London.

The 7th Earl Stanhope, being last of the line, set up a trust in 1959 by which the estate is managed by trustees and it is the Prime Minister who nominates a resident of the house. This resident must be either a cabinet minister or a lineal descendent of George I. Between 1974 and 1980 this was the Prince of Wales; at the time of writing it is the foreign secretary, Jack Straw.

In the weeks before Christmas a six-pointed star blazes from the hill behind Chevening. The huge wood-framed star is raised by tractor and pulley up the side of their house by Mr Viner and his wife to celebrate Advent. Their house was formerly the Star pub on Star Hill. Each year Mr and Mrs Viner receive letters of appreciation from children who see the star from the motorway. These letters are often addressed simply to 'The Man with the Star', but with no further information are safely delivered by the Post Office.

Squerryes

Squerryes estate is the last in Kent, being in Westerham, the westernmost village, on the A25. The Warde family have been the owners since 1731, when the house was 45 years old. The first two Wardes made their fortunes as

Squerryes

silk and cloth merchants trading with Flanders. Both Sir Patience and Sir John became Lord Mayors of London. Sir John took the side of parliament in the Civil War, escaped to Flanders on the Restoration and had to buy a pardon from Charles II to return. This pardon, in 'chancery-hand' as Pepys calls it, is displayed in the house. Also on display are General Wolfe's army commission and the letter written by Pitt to Wolfe's mother after his death. Why the Wolfe memorabilia? Because his house, Quebec House, was just across the field from the rear of Squerryes. It is now National Trust and, like Squerryes, is open.❀

Youngsters perch on the great man's lap, Westerham Green

Many other famous names are linked with Westerham: Churchill (at Chartwell nearby)❀, Pitt the Younger (for whom Lady Hester Stanhope of Chevening, afterwards the great traveller 'Queen Hester' of the Lebanon, kept house), John Frith, the biblical scholar, Hansard of the parliamentary reports and even Alice Hargreaves, who spent her last years here: *née* Alice Liddell, she was the Alice of the Looking Glass.

Of the many roads that pass over this stretch of the M25, one brought the Battle of Britain pilots down from Biggin Hill to the 'unofficial Officers' Mess', the White Hart at Brasted. A photograph of a blackboard signed by them hangs in the pub (the original is with the Museum of London).

Titsey

Titsey Place is approximately a mile north and west of the services, just left of the prominent church. Sir John Gresham bought the estate in 1535. His elder brother Richard founded the family fortunes by hiring vessels and trading on his own account. Richard was Lord Mayor in

Titsey, home of the Gresham family

1537, John in 1547. Most famous was Sir Thomas, Richard's son, who became Elizabeth's agent and spy master in the Low Countries. He was also a banker and, inspired by the Amsterdam Exchange built the Exchange in London – a courtyard open to the sky so that all transactions should be under the eye of God. The original building was later destroyed in the Great Fire. Gresham also built a mansion at Osterley Park, acquired three other country estates, endowed a grammar school in Norfolk and, by bequest, founded Gresham College, then the only college outside Oxbridge. There is still a Gresham Street in the City. It is one-way and I can never find the right end of it! The Gresham family crest was a grasshopper, carved on the front of Titsey, which became the symbol of a national bank until amalgamations in the 1970's. The Greshams continued to live at Titsey until 1804 when the male line ended and Katherine Gresham married William Leveson Gower. In 1979 the last Leveson Gowers set up a trust to preserve the estate for the public. ❀

In reaching Titsey we have passed the Kent/Surrey border and Clacket Services. The latter was named after Clackett's Lane, a humble country road.
Local people insist on retaining the full spelling of Clackett's where the motorway is succeeding in reducing it to Clacket. Running through the lorry parks both sides of the motorway north-south was found a Roman road. This led from London to the great ironworks in the Sussex Forest. Many thousands of slaves were no

Clacket Lane on a good day

Overleaf: Titsey South Lodge

doubt marched down the hill here and off to the south to a miserable existence. A small temple was found just north of the Services and several finds are exhibited on the north side.

Just after the Services northside, difficult to see clockwise, but very prominent anti, is Titsey South Lodge. Before it lies its small but impeccably-kept garden. It is the home of Richard and Doreen Abbott, now retired from work on the estate. Richard's father was gamekeeper, living in a cottage amongst the trees at Clackett's. No road or lane led to the cottage, merely a muddy path. At that spot now is the busiest road in Europe. Richard is now so used to the road, he ignores it, adjusting his voice without thinking to the volume of the traffic. Did it ever disturb them? Yes, one night, he said,

there was a tremendous bang which woke us up. We got out of bed to see, if there was a crash, if we could help. There was nothing to be seen except a large lorry parked on the hard shoulder on the opposite side of the motorway. We went back to bed. In the morning the lorry was gone but at the foot of the garden some fifteen foot below the M25 was an enormous wheel. It must have come off the lorry, crossed the central reservation and motorway fence to end up at the bottom of the bank. Nobody claimed it.

After Titsey northside is the great quarry. In fact there are several along the escarpment but most are now so overgrown that they appear merely as woods. This one, operated by Tilcon produces chalk for agricultural use in two grades. The kilns formerly used to produce lime are still there, having been listed. The quarry is worked subject to its ultimate re-instatement as a natural feature, and so every lorry that comes for chalk brings with it a load of soil

Kilns at Titsey

which is bulldozed into a great ramp obvious from the road.

The slight cutting at this point marks the spot where the Greenwich meridian intersects the road, so you are due south of the observatory. On the northern sector the meridian passes through Waltham Abbey, where a brass rod in the abbey grounds places it exactly.

Just after the quarry the Brighton railway emerges from a tunnel north to burrow under the M25. Richard Abbott's father reckoned that the building of this tunnel reduced the flow in the springs behind Titsey which had until then been the main source of the Darenth.

If you could go through the railway tunnel, it would be the quickest way to get to Marden, a part of Godstone but now severed from it by the M25. Evelyn's diary records:

With Sir Robert Clayton to Marden, an estate he

had lately bought of my kindsman Sir John Evelyn of Godstone in Surrey: which from a despicable farme house Sir Robert had erected into a Seate with extraordinary expense.

About the same time (1677) Sir Robert bought Bletchingley from the Mordaunts, a story we come to shortly. He was a banker, Lord Mayor in 1679 and MP for the city twice. Having bought Bletchingley, a notorious rotten borough, he was MP for another three terms, as well as a director of the new Bank of England, governor of the Irish Society, vice-president of the London Workhouse and president of St Thomas' Hospital. Macaulay describes Clayton as Lord Mayor as 'all over scarlet and ermine and half over diamonds',

the wealthiest merchant of London, whose palace in the Old Jewry surpasses in splendour the aristocratical mansions of Lincolns Inn Fields and Covent Garden, whose villa amongst the Surrey hills was described as a Garden of Eden, whose banquets vied with those of kings, and whose judicious munificence, still attested by numerous public monuments, had obtained for him in the annals of the City a place second only to that of Gresham.

Sir Robert Clayton

Was it by chance that these banking families lived so close? Sir Robert can still be seen in an alabaster monument in Bletchingley church, with his wife, pointing to their only child, who died in infancy. Sacheverell Sitwell called the tomb

the finest monument of the Baroque in England... one of the most entirely satisfying works of art in the whole kingdom.

You will be lucky to get a clear view of it uncluttered by parochial noticeboards.

Sir Robert's house did not survive. The mansion was knocked down and replaced by a large red-brick building in the 1880's by the

Society of the Sacred Heart who used it as a Catholic girls' school. Eventually they left and it became, as now, interdenominational. However the site is as impressive as ever. The visitor follows a twisting drive for about a mile before, with a final turn, he finds himself suddenly before a huge building enclosed by steep slopes. This is now **Woldingham School**. Sir Robert would have found the railway station just outside his gates very convenient for the City. Also less dangerous, as Evelyn relates of his journeying up the A22 just short of Bromley:

As I rod negligently under favour of the shade… started out two Cutthroates and striking with their long staves at the horse, taking hold of the reignes, threw me down and immediately took my sworde and haled me into a deep thickett some quarter of a mile from the highway where they might securely rob me.

A more recent financier living just south of the motorway along here is **Mr Al Fayed**, the owner of Harrods, who travels safely to work by helicopter. When at home (Barrow Green Court) he operates out of a tent in the garden. By coincidence his house was once lived in by Jeremy Bentham, who had himself mummified, an outcome Fayed has claimed to be planning for himself (together with a glass pyramid on the roof of his shop, so that he, like Bentham, can be enjoyed by visitors). A second Roman road descended the hill here, heading for Lewes.

Just north of J6, obvious anti but needing a sharp turn of the head clockwise, is Godstone Vineyard. It is actually at the mouth of an enormous quarry, long disused and masked by trees. Access is by Quarry Lane, using the first gap in the dual carriageway from the A22 north. The public are welcome at any time to walk round the vines.✿ During the summer one can sit with a drink on the verandah of the Vineyard Restaurant and watch the traffic stream by. Not for the only time does one find oneself thinking how peaceful this scene must have been before the motorway was built.

Just south of J6 amongst the trees is the Kent and Surrey police control for the motorway between the River Crossing and J12. There are three others: from Heston on the M4, the Metropolitan, Surrey and Thames Valley forces control J12 to J17; from Welwyn the Hertfordshire police control J17 to J23; from Chigwell the Metropolitan and Essex forces control J23 back to the Crossing. If you cannot see them, they certainly can see you via the

Godstone Police Centre

video cameras along the road. If for any reason you dial 999 on your mobile on the M25, you will be put through to one of these centres who will take your report and then ring you back to confirm your identity.

After the police wood south is a round-topped hill barely discernible from the motor-

way. It is a large bronze-age tumulus behind the village of Godstone. Beyond this, still southside, is a long low farmhouse opposite two grey barns at right angles to the road. This was originally the family home of the entertainer Richard Stilgoe but due to his efforts is now the centre of the Orpheus Trust —

a place where disabled and non-disabled people can spend time together creating music, drama, songs, stories, and art, and show the rest of the world just how excellent the human race can be.

The Orpheus Trust

Eight helpers ('enablers'), two professionals, and a permanent staff take twelve students (disabled) for courses of a day, a week, or a fortnight to prepare a public performance. The membership of the Trust's council reads like a Who's Who of top British theatre people. The

extension of the original building was completed in 1998. The result is, in scale, friendly, in practice, efficient, in purpose, outstandingly altruistic.✿

Several road bridges span the M25 between J6 and J7. The last leads to Buckingham Palace, a few yards from the motorway. It is the second of the disappearing palaces. The de Stafford family were made Dukes of Buckingham in 1444. The palace was built in 1517, two years after Otford, probably by the same craftsmen. It was similar in form, with buildings surrounding two courtyards with a strong gatehouse. The fifth Duke was executed by Henry VIII for plotting treason

in the gallery of his palace at Bletchingley.

Afterwards Henry gave the palace to Anne of Cleves who lived there until 1547. Elizabeth gave it to the Howard family whose most illustrious member was the admiral who defeated the Armada and led the raid on Cádiz.

Inheriting the property, the admiral's daughter married John Mordaunt, Earl of Peterborough. Their son Henry far outdid Douglas Fairbanks Jnr. in his life of action, but ended up heavily in debt by gambling in the lax days of the Restoration. He sold Bletchingley to Sir Robert Clayton and, although it was probably done quite formally in the City, I like to think of him trotting on his horse round the hill at J6 to see Sir Robert about it. The old palace was of no interest to its new owner. It seems that it was allowed to fall to bits. Now only remnants of the walls survive in barns and the gatehouse became part of a farmhouse. Quite recently the wall behind the classical front porch was laid bare and the original Tudor arch revealed. It was yet another Mordaunt who came across Earl Stanhope in Spain. Stanhope being swarthy was nicknamed 'The Don'. Mordaunt made this into Don Quixote, which brought a challenge to a duel, prevented only by the high command. The M25 runs actually through the deer park of the palace to which Henry III gave ten hinds and two stags in 1233.

Buckingham Palace, doorway and its 18th century improvement

The park had disappeared and become six separate farms by 1680, when the remains are referred to as

an ancient dyke and bank of earth on which formerly stood the park pale.

The village of Bletchingley up on the hill to the south is well worth a visit, an illustrated

Overleaf: The medieval High Street, Bletchingley

guide being available from the post office.
Bletchingley was created a borough in about
1200, the local lord marking out plots to let to
craftsmen and merchants who would develop
the village and thereby increase the value of
the lord's estate. These plots ran either side of
the main street, now
Church Walk, and
there was a market
place to the rear
where the A25 now
runs through the vil-
lage. We have, there-
fore, to thank the
market place for the
preservation of this
ancient main street,
traffic preferring the
easier route.

Water tower, Gravelly Hill

North of the M25
after J6 is seen
Gravelly Hill, wooded and with a prominent
water tower. Site of a stone-age fortification,

the area is being developed by its council as a public open space.✿ Near the summit is a viewpoint with map and, surprisingly, one looks straight down the valley to **Gatwick Airport** where aircraft can be seen moving about the runway.

The water tower resembles a rook from a chess set (as does the tower by J24). It was built of brick in 1897; the top two of its five stories are taken up by a metal water tank. Access to the roof with its mobile phone aerials is via a ladder which leads up through a tube in the centre of the tank.✿

The small brick building north immediately before J7 is a gas pipeline station.

Over the Chalk
Again
J7 to J9

THE M25 RISES TO ITS HIGHEST POINT — some 700 feet (215 m) — at the top of Reigate Hill. At J7 traffic from the M23 enters, pushing into the middle lanes for the run up the hill, while vehicles on the motorway

Description J7–J9

are moving left to access the slip. To the north is a steep, ploughed hill on which tractors look decidedly precarious. To the south, invisible from the motorway, is the old village of Merstham. The ancient road from Merstham runs next to the M25 up the hill. Beyond it are Reigate Golf Club and higher up, amongst the trees, Gatton. After the summit the road descends mainly through cuttings to J9.

Apart from the occasional glimpse of rural valleys to the north this section offers nothing but seven miles of tedium. At the foot of the hill, the chalky banks vanish. Forty miles or one third of the M25 have been travelled either on or looking up at chalk. There is now no more until J30!

Previous pages: Motorway rising towards Reigate Hill, looking clockwise

THE PRESENT ROUTE was certainly not the one favoured by the engineers. As at Darenth

Construction J7-J9

they preferred to work where the land was level, which meant a route south of **Reigate** and **Dorking**. Local opposition was vehement. Check any bookshop; if there is one book on **Kent** or **Cornwall**, there will be ten on **Surrey**. These people are literate and loquacious. The **Planning Officer** at the **Public Enquiry** felt called upon to say:

> It is not an edifying spectacle to see groups of professional, intellectual and articulate people, behaving at times as an unruly mob.

There was no way through the valley; the road had to be cut through the chalk. The task was not as great as at Darenth: where Darenth cost £30 million, J8 to J9 cost £14 million. There are in fact only two hills on the southern section of the M25, a fact which affects one's driving considerably. Lorries do not block the motorway with their overtaking manoeuvres

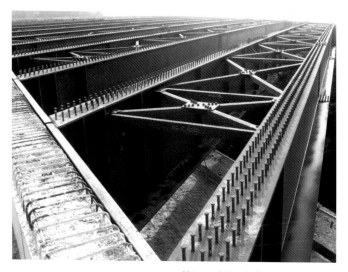

Motorway bridge decking prior to concreting

nearly as often as on the northern section.
I once asked a haulier why lorry drivers strug-
gled in these pitifully slow overtakes. 'Got to
keep the revs up,' he said. 'Keep the revs up.'

The pedestrian girder bridges between J7
and J8 were delivered in one piece, which
meant that the motorway was closed for one

day while they were lifted into position. All the bridges on the M25 were built originally wide enough to accommodate four lanes, although now on the widened sections their supports intrude upon the hard shoulder. Pollution control valves beside the road serve the same purpose (removing dirty water) as the lagoons met with earlier.

TO THE SOUTH OF J7 and west of the M23 lies the village of Merstham. In this area was  found many centuries ago a limestone ideal for building. It was used for London Bridge, Windsor Castle and Henry VII's Chapel in Westminster Abbey. The great problem with both chalk and and stone was one of transport. The following was written of a road in Essex in 1769:

It is for 12 miles so narrow that a mouse cannot pass by any carriage. I saw a fellow creep under his

waggon to assist me to lift, if possible, my chaise
over a hedge... to add to all the infamous circum-
stances which concur to plague a traveller I must
not forget the eter-
nally meeting with
chalk waggons, them-
selves frequently
stuck fast till a collec-
tion of them are in the same situation and twenty
or thirty horses may be tacked to each other to
draw them out one by one.

17th century waggon

**Eventually the problem in Merstham was
solved by the opening of the Grand Surrey Iron
Railway which used horse-drawn trucks and
was extended from Wandsworth to Merstham
in 1816.**

**On fine Sundays not so long ago it was the
custom for people from Reigate and Merstham
to walk to the top of the hill in the afternoon.
There they could buy refreshments and enjoy
the views. The M25 has put paid to that!
Amongst the trees on the summit of Reigate
Hill southside, that is above the golf course, is**

Gatton Hall. Built by W. J. Manson in a classical style, it was notorious before the Reform Bill of 1832 as a borough returning two MP's while often having a constituency of only one — the owner. To add to the farce a gazebo in the form of a small Greek temple some 20 foot by 10 was set up in front of the Hall in 1765 and christened Gatton Town Hall. There elections were solemnly conducted. At the turn of the century the Hall was inhabited by Jeremiah Colman of mustard fame, but was then deserted after punitive death duties. Gutted by fire in the 1920's, it was used as a billet for Canadians during WWII. Now it forms the centre of a group of buildings used by the Royal Alexandra and Albert School. The diminutive town hall still stands, now a listed building.✿

North of the M25 between J8 and J9 one sees on the map names such as Kingswood the Forest, Buckland and Prince's Covert, all testifying to the royal interest in hunting in this area. In fact Henry VIII built two palaces to

Gatton Town Hall

Nonsuch in 1513; it was eventually given to Charles II's mistress and sold as building materials

indulge his hobby in his royal forests. The first, Nonsuch, near Sutton, has been excavated and found to be slightly smaller than the

archbishop's at Otford (see p. 82); the second, Oatlands, near Weybridge, was grander and used by the Stuarts. It was Cromwell who had its value assessed as both a complete building and as a source of building materials. It was sold as the latter for £4933.90.

The royal forests, in case the reader has not come across them before, were more than stretches of woodland. Any area could be legally 'afforested' or 'disafforested' by the Crown. In the first case farmers could farm and villagers use the common land within these areas but none was allowed to enclose land and impede the King's hunting. Other rules were imposed regarding how trees might be cut and dogs allowed to run. The enforcement of these rules by courts of Verderers led to fines being imposed and money raised for the Crown. (A bit like parking meters actually.) What happened on disafforestation we shall see at Epping (p. 269).

Unenclosed, the heaths of Banstead north of

the motorway became a pleasure ground for Londoners. When Pepys proudly bought his first coach and pair, it was to Banstead that he drove his wife at the weekend. Evelyn's wife had worse luck:

> My wife going into Surry, the Axletree of the Coach firing on Banstead Downe, they endeavoured to quench it with the fat of the meate was carried with them and a bottle of sack, to refresh them on the way, no water neere them til they came to Leatherhead.

After the Restoration, Epsom and its wells became a fashionable resort and soon after a racing centre, the Derby being instituted in 1756. Finally, also on the north side, why should a hamlet of a pub and a dozen houses be called Mogador, a name found otherwise in Morocco? It is suggested that there was at one time living there a Sir Richard Maggot, his house being called 'Maggot Hall'. Over the years this became corrupted, quite understandably, to 'Mogador'.

South of the M25 lies Headley Court, a large RAF establishment for the convalescence of airmen and surrounded by MoD 'Keep Out' notices. At a couple of points narrow bridges cross the motorway and here, with no escape but upwards, the traffic noise is intense. However there is very little to interest the motorist through these seven miles of cuttings down to J9.

Returning from the Derby, 1872

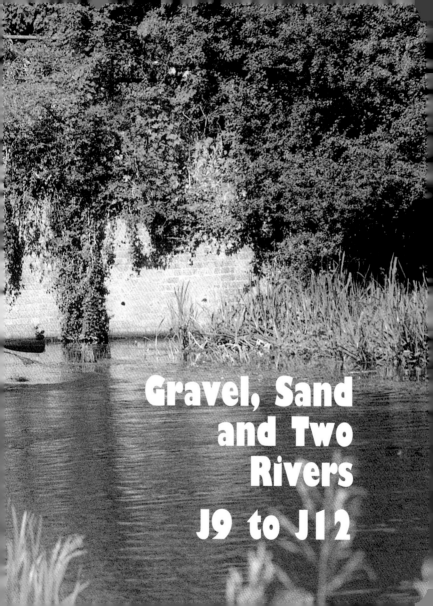

Gravel, Sand
and Two
Rivers
J9 to J12

THE SPLIT JUNCTION J9 was so built as not to disturb the residents of Leatherhead to the south or Ashstead to the north. Embankments on both sides therefore isolate the road for two miles. Thereafter the River

Description J9-J12

Mole appears southside and passes to and fro under the M25 three times before going off to West and East Molesey to join the Thames directly opposite Hampton Court. On its bend to the north of the road, prominent anti-clockwise, difficult to see clockwise, are the manor house and church of Stoke d'Abernon. Screen fencing then becomes more general. The London-Guildford railway is crossed. Approaching J10 sand and gravel banks rise both sides, surmounted by silver birch woods. Over the trees southside, parallel with the final gantry before J10, may just be seen the tip of a metal wing, of which more later. J10 to J11 is almost totally fenced, only asphalt surfaces, 'blacktop' in the jargon, occurring amongst the general concrete to betray the presence of

Previous pages: On the Wey

The M25 being built top left to bottom right to share the narrow gap north of Leatherhead with the Leatherhead by-pass (seen winding in and out and still in use)

bridges beneath. **The road rises gradually to pass over the Wey Canal a mile before J11. The point at which it does so (at the New Haw Viaduct) is given away by the asphalt, the lower fences each side, the double bang of your** vehicle crossing the expansion joints and, finally, by the great wires of the National Grid passing over on pylons. The fencing continues between J11 and J12. A rounded hill with three trees is seen southside opposite a much larger hill north and then a concrete railway bridge.

AS THE INHABITANTS OF SURREY would not have the M25 go south of Leatherhead and Dorking, it had to pass through the quarter mile gap between the two towns of Ashstead and Leatherhead. This space was already occupied by the Leatherhead by-pass. The result was another M25 compromise, both roads running parallel, access by one half junction, egress by another. High earth banks and extensive planting were added to protect the residents from noise. These banks were grassed by using 'grobags' whose rectangular shape is still to be seen. These measures were guaranteed to give local inhabitants a

Construction J9-J12

reduction of 15% in pollution and 15 decibels in noise nuisance. During the widening to four lanes, 550,000 more trees and shrubs were planted. Where the M25 completely disrupted local traffic, new minor roads were built.

Also on this section appear the first automatic speed limit gantries. Those who marvel at the brightness of these signs, even in full sunlight, might be surprised to learn that the light source of each sign is a single 150 watt bulb feeding a bunch of glass fibres. Designed to prevent the stop/go progress of slowing traffic, the variable speed limits depend on the cooperation of drivers. No more need be said.

J10 is the first of seven junctions where the inside lane is lost to traffic leaving the motorway, and regained after the junction. In light traffic conditions this system is effective, in peak hours rather less so. Slow traffic moves into the second lane about a mile before the junction, reducing to two the lanes available to cars. God forbid that one slow vehicle now overtakes another at this point because then only one lane remains for cars. J10 to J16 is best avoided in both directions during the rush hours.

The New Haw Viaduct, as the big bridge is known between J10 and J11 is, after the Gade Valley Viaduct and the River Crossing, the greatest feat of engineering on the M25. It crosses both the Wey Navigation Canal and the London to Woking railway, is 935 feet (285 m) long with eight spans on seven huge concrete legs, and it cost £3.7 million.

The extraordinary feature of the $2^1/_2$ mile section between J11 and J12 is the concrete railway bridge over the motorway. This has to be the ugliest edifice of the M25. The towers rise 90 foot above the motorway to carry, via suspension cables, a pre-stressed concrete bridge, the whole thing being set at an angle to accommodate the track. It was designed by BR and looks decidedly retro.

Overleaf: The railway bridge between J11 and J12

AFTER J9 THE M25 is again crossing manorial lands, here the manor of Ashstead, as Leatherhead was until the recent past only a small village on the Mole. The manor house is a classic case of a Stuart house replacing an Elizabethan which was allowed to fall down, and then the Stuart itself being demolished a hundred years later to make way for the new classical style. The Lords of the Manor were again the Howard family. Several of the family, by the way, are in portraits in the Ranger's House, Blackheath (another Stanhope house) the admiral not looking a robust man but with small effeminate hands. In 1889 on the death of the last Howard owner, Ashstead House was put up for sale as

Background J9-J12

a palatial mansion standing in a majestically timbered deer park of 200 acres.

The estate was sold to a banker and broken up; but Ashstead Common was another piece of ancient woodland saved, like Epping (J27) and Burnham Beeches (J16) by the Corporation of the City of London.

A fascinating place adjacent to J9 is the Fire and Iron Gallery. It is only feet from the motorway, the mere mention of which here caused a look of bitterness on the faces of those affected, as I have noticed all round the M25. The Gallery houses a very large collection of works of art in metal, all for sale, and has several blacksmiths at work on the site. Of their many commissions perhaps the most notable were the gates of the Globe Theatre on Bankside, the work of many artists brought together.✿

The Fire and Iron Gallery: the motorway gantries can be seen behind the sculpture

The Mole has its source in the eastern border of Worth Forest, near Turner's Hill where

Sir John d'Abernon, 1277

rise three rivers within a few hundred yards of each other, flowing north and east and south: the Mole, the Medway and the Ouse. Here the Mole crosses a flat area, and during the last few winters the Mole has regularly flooded the fields beside it. On the north side, soon after J9, the river makes a lovely setting for the manor house and church of Stoke d'Abernon, prominent anti-clockwise.

The manor belonged to one of William I's knights, Sir Roger d'Abernon, and a brass of his descendant, Sir John

(d. 1277), is thought to be the oldest in the country. Parts of the church are Saxon from about 600 AD. There are many other interesting features but they are only to be seen by the public on Sunday afternoons. The manor house is a preparatory school for boys. On entering the building one is struck by the warm and welcoming attitude of all within it. Except one. Having made myself known to the secretary I had a quick look round the outside of the church. Looking every day at things from the M25, it is fascinating to find yourself looking the other way, back at the motorway. There it was, streaming past. However, every time I turned round, I saw a man's head disappear behind a rose bush. The caretaker was convinced he had a paedophile on the loose.

Just before J10 southside a metal sail, the 'wing' mentioned earlier, may be seen sticking up above the trees. It is of course more easily seen in winter and from the anticlockwise direction. The trees themselves are on Ockham Common, an area of sand and gravel

where only trees such as birch can grow. In fact it is hoped by the conservators that all these trees will eventually be replaced by open heathland such as was thought to exist years ago. The metal sail or wing is part of the semaphore apparatus on top of Chatley Heath Semaphore Tower. This is a 5-storey red brick hexagonal tower, built in 1822, a survivor of the 19 built between London and Portsmouth. It was claimed that officers on the towers, by manipulating the semaphore arms, could send messages between the port and the Admiralty in 15 minutes. Access to the tower is via the A3 (south) and the first turn left. ✿

   On the opposite side of the motorway and only yards from it is Painshill Park. It has to be reached by the usual circuitous route (leave at J10, take the A3 north, and follow the signs). Painshill occupies about 1 1/4 miles of the Mole valley, more than half of it being flooded to form a lake with islets. It was created as a romantic landscape, one of the first in this

Semaphore tower   *Overleaf: the lake at Painshill Park*

fashion, by the Hon. Charles Hamilton between 1738 and 1773. Although almost destroyed by neglect after WWII, the park is now in the care of trustees and volunteers who are continually at work on its restoration, earning in 1998 the Europa Nostra medal

for the exemplary restoration... of a most important 18th century landscape park and its extraordinary buildings.

There are in fact a dozen buildings such as a ruined abbey, a Gothick tower and a Turkish tent which, constructed out of wood or brick but rendered to look like stone in the manner of stage scenery, draw the eye to focal points in the scenery. Painshill Park was conceived in days pre-postcard and pre-photography; it is delightful. The guide book at £3.50 is a must.✿

Just after J10 southside, signposted from the A3 is Wisley, headquarters of the Royal Horticultural Society whose gardens are open all year. ✿ How is so much grown in such a dry place? I was told that the Gardens may take 4 million gallons annually from the Wey, after which they have to rely on their own bore-holes. Woefully igno-rant of the flora, I examined the fauna to find that they were our antipodean cousins, armed with shears and forks and flourishing in the northern latitudes. Following the narrow road from the Gardens through Wisley village you come to Pyrford Lock on the canal, postcard pretty with a pub which does food.

Wisley: the Country Garden

North of the M25 and no distance from it is Brooklands. To say that this racing circuit, built 1907, is 3¼ miles long, 100 feet wide and banked to 29 degrees gives little idea of the abnormality of this track. Five concrete slabs each 20 feet wide are laid at increasingly steep angles to the height of a house, to form a wall of death on a grand scale. Flyers soon moved in to use the level sections of track as runways. Vickers appeared in 1912. When motor racing ceased in 1939, it was never to return. Aircraft production, particularly of Hurricanes and Wellingtons during the war, took over, which in its turn ceased in 1989.

My first attempt to find Brooklands ended in a supermarket carpark, and while I sat musing on the obscurity of maps and the impatience of local drivers who bully anyone unsure of his way, I noticed that the supermarket had a most peculiar wall round it. I was as surprised as Thisbe... This was the track, and I was inside it, as were a dozen factories, and the Brooklands Motor Museum.✿

Halfway between J10 and J11, another revolution in transport was signalled by the Wey Navigation, the first of three canals encountered on the M25. It was built by Act of

Brooklands: the track and the supermarket carpark both clearly visible

Parliament in 1651 to join the Thames with Guildford, and used materials from Oatlands Palace. In 1816 the route was extended via the Arun Canal to Portsmouth. There was even

New Haw Viaduct

talk of enlargement in 1830 to a Grand Naval
Canal by which warships might be moved
between Portsmouth and the Thames. The
Wey Navigation closed commercially in 1969
and is now in the care of the National Trust
and used by pleasure craft.

The New Haw Viaduct over the canal is sup-
ported on seven giant concrete legs gratefully
received by local spray artists. Standing

beneath the motorway, with the traffic hitting the expansion joints, one hears a succession of booms like a hi-fi at full stretch; lying calmly tied to the canal bank are Peggotty, Malaga Fred, and the Lady of Shalott.

Past J11 southside is Cockcrow Hill, a prominent round knoll surmounted by three trees and now with a model railway complete with station running round its base.✿ The Great Cockrow Railway, for such it is called, runs for

Great Cockrow Railway

2$^1/_2$ miles through 4 acres; it is owned and operated by a club of 35 enthusiasts who offer steam journeys to the public but in the summer months only.

Although Cockrow Hill is shaped like a tumulus, I was assured by its owner that it is completely natural. Said owner lives in a fine seventeenth century brick farmhouse tucked away on the far side of the hill. Invited to the top of the hill which I see most days of my life while working, it seemed once again odd to be looking the other way.

The much larger hill on the other side of the M25 is St Anne's, named after a church of which hardly anything remains. This hill is the site of a bronze-age fort but now has a few select residences (one of which was owned by the statesman Fox), a nature trail, viewpoints and a dingle. Indeed the hill is much larger than it appears from the M25, although locals complain that much of it was taken for the building of the motorway. Both Cockcrow and

St Anne's are, of course in Chertsey. It is the
M25 which leads one to think of Chertsey as
north of the motorway only.

Gravel and
Water
J12 to J16

BETWEEN J12 AND J13, where the road is occasionally unfenced, there are pleasant views of old gravel workings now flooded to form lakes. On the hill west can be seen a Victorian red brick building with a tower. At J13, with the

Description
J12-J16

slip roads on both sides level with the motorway, the M25 passes over the Thames. Clockwise one has to look for the old-fashioned stone balustrades, anti-clockwise the river can be seen beyond the concrete.

The barren gravel soil around Heathrow makes a dismal scene, cheered only by areas of improvement by the local authority. Only from the rising sliproads feeding the M4 at J15 are there panoramic views, but there is little time to take them in. From J13 to J17 the M25 runs through the Colne Valley Park. As in the Lea Valley and, to a lesser extent, the Darenth Valley, local authorities have established visitors' centres, cleared lakes and restored

J12, the M25/M3 junction

footpaths for recreational use. Immediately after J15 east is Thorney Country Park, part of Colne Valley with two lakes, Thorney Deep and Larbourne Pond.✿ After them come a school and a golf club. After one mile from J15 the M25 crosses the Maidenhead railway and Grand Union Canal (Slough Branch), both hidden by fencing. There are then fields both sides with a view to Uxbridge east. At J16 one can look briefly east and west along the M40.

AT J12 THERE WERE NO PROBLEMS with intersecting the M3 with a multi-level free-flow interchange. Crossing the  Thames at J13 was a different matter. Between the reservoirs and rivers only a narrow neck of land was available and this was already occupied by the A30 Staines by-pass. Staines in fact, was known to the Romans as Pontes or Bridges, probably because with few houses and several rivers converging on it, the view was

Lutyens bridge and copy. Overleaf, the same bridges seen from the towpath

one of bridges everywhere – just like **Bruges** in **Belgium**. **Before the WWII the A30 crossed the Thames by a bridge in Staines town centre; it still does but in 1960 this was by-passed by the building of a beautiful brick bridge designed by Lutyens (who had been a consult-ant on one of the original plans for a London ring road). As the Lutyens bridge could take only five lanes of traffic and there was no other land available, it was decided to build another, identical structure but in concrete beside the**

original. Each bridge was then to take M25 plus A30 traffic in each direction. Both bridges may be viewed at close quarters by taking the road to Runnymede off J13 and walking back along the towpath.

The section J14 to J15 was expensive to construct owing to the need for a four-level free-flow interchange between the M25 and M4. Massive embankments were needed to build the slip roads, but they had the problem, more familiar in Holland, of flat country with no earth to hand. Three and a half million cubic metres of soil had to be transported to the site, much of it from St Anne's Hill. The extravagance here may be compared with the parsimony at one of the main links to the continent, J2 at Dartford, which was built for £3 million, where great trucks negotiate a roundabout with traffic lights and where, if any vehicle suffers a puncture, a four mile queue forms within minutes.

J15 shortly after construction: the M4 passing left to right under the M25 and slip roads

Between J15 and J16 an asbestos tip had to be covered with a concrete platform before the M25 could proceed. The complexity of J16, the M40 interchange, was so great that like J13 at Runnymede, it was awarded a separate contract, the carriageway either side not being part of it. It was kept down to two levels, its links and loops hidden by banking.

At £21 million it was half the cost of J15 but 450,000 cubic metres of spoil were moved and 186,000 trees and shrubs planted.

EAST OF J12-J13 is Thorpe which, like Egham, belonged to the **Abbots of Chertsey**. Now best  known for its water park in old gravel workings, there is also an old and handsome village of Thorpe. Amongst many red brick buildings are the **Red Lion** (1700) and **Thorpe Place** (1801), which is now occupied by **TASIS**, the American School in Switzerland.

Just after Longside Lake westside is Great Fosters, now a hotel but formerly the home of Sir John Dodderidge, Solicitor General to James I, and after 1630, of Sir Robert Foster, Lord Chief Justice under Charles II. For good food in a great atmosphere the hotel can be recommended. Beyond Great Fosters and Egham are the meadows of Runnymede with the Magna Carta monument (paid for by Americans) and the J. F. Kennedy memorial.❀ Just above is the Air Forces Memorial, to airmen who have no known grave.❀ Silhouetted on the hill one sees the tower of a Victorian sanatorium, now converted to private flats, and below it the buildings of Holloway College, founded as a college for young ladies by Sir Thomas Holloway, a patent medicine magnate, in 1875. The architecture

The Magna Carta monument

was inspired by the Château de Chambord in the Loire valley – a spectacular concatenation of turrets, towers and chimneys.✿

Between J13 and J14 the story is one of water. Here six rivers have converged: Thames, Colne, Chess, Gade, Misbourne and Wraysbury. In 1792 Archibald Robertson wrote:

> Notwithstanding the ample manner by which London and its suburbs are supplied with water from the River Lea and the Thames, a scheme was some time ago in contemplation to convey a part of the River Colne to the western division of the metropolis.

In fact the proposal to bring water to the City via Brentford dated from 1580 but was never carried out. London was supplied from a couple of streams which ran through it, wells dug by the citizens, and water brought up from the Thames by paddle wheels on London Bridge. The present scheme of reservoirs dates from 1898. Water is pumped from the Thames at Hythe End (J13) into six huge reservoirs: Staines (1) and Staines (2) finished 1902, Queen Mary 1925, George VI 1947, Wraysbury 1971, Queen Mother 1975. An aqueduct leads from these to purification works at Hampton and thence to the London Ring Main, which serves four million customers.

By J13 is Bell Weir. In winter you may find a rowing eight out training or a runner or

The Thames at Runnymede

mountain biker on the footpath. There was more happening in 1792:

> The Thames being the grand channel of communication from the interior parts of England lying west from the capital, an immense trade in corn, timber and other merchandise is constantly carried on by its means.

To reach the Thames from J13 going clockwise, leave on the slip road, descend to the roundabout and go all the way round it until you rise again on the slip road beside the M25 going in the opposite direction; keep to the left until you reach another roundabout; take the third exit for Runnymede. There is a car park and 'pleasure ground' about one mile along on your right. It's worth it!

There are several interesting villages either side of the M25. Poyle, owned by the painter of miniatures Nicholas Hilliard under Elizabeth I, is now submerged beneath a trading estate, but Colnbrook and Longford have fared better.

Both were stopping places on the old Bath road with coaching inns and tales of a revolving bed which 'done in' the traveller while he slept. Then comes Heathrow, first mentioned as a village on the edge of Hounslow Heath in 1453. It can never have been rich: Cobbett described the heath as

a nasty strong dirt upon a bed of gravel and is a sample of all that is bad and villainous in look.

These spaces were used by Charles II to quarter his army, close enough, he thought, to threaten, sufficiently far off not to annoy the people of London. He was mistaken; the population of the city flowed out to cater for the wants of the camp and it became something of a fair.

In 1784 General Roy settled on the area as suitable for measuring a base line over five miles of flat country to establish the relative positions of the London and Paris observatories, an exercise that would eventually form the basis of the Ordnance Survey. Using 20 foot long glass tubes, not subject to the expansion/contraction of metal, he measured out a distance of 27,404.01 (sic) feet between Heathrow and Hampton. Waggon wheels were buried at each end of the line, but as they rotted they were replaced by cannon buried vertically. One of these cannon may be seen, painted silver, in a small garden on the corner of the police pound on the Heathrow perimeter road, adjacent to the traffic lights. It is the ancestor of all scientific maps of this country, including the ones in this book.

Heathrow was then left to itself. Despite Cobbett's remarks on the soil, it did well in market gardening, the carts taking produce into London returning with ample horse manure from the horse-drawn traffic. But this rural life during the 1930's suffered two invasions. First aircraft. Both manufacturers and their customers were looking for room

General Roy's cannon and commemorative plaque, Heathrow

Heathrow in the Iron Age: a reconstruction

close to London and four small airfields were
established, Heston, Fairey's, Heathrow and
Hawkers. As Fairey's grew, it became the
'Harmondsworth Aerodrome' and then the
'Great West Aerodrome'. Between 1935 and
1939 this became the venue for the Royal
Aeronautical Society's garden party. The
commercial airport of London at that time

was Croydon. H.V. Morton gives a taste of the age:

This is the Control Tower of London's Airport. It is the ear, eye, and voice of the aerodrome. There is nothing else like it in the country. Pilots in the clouds above the Channel pour their troubles into the ears behind the headphones, and voices from this white tower go out into the sky, soothing the worries of airmen in bad weather, helping them, leading them home. On a cork table is painted a map of Europe. One of the men is always busy sticking little coloured flags on the map. 'Look,' he says 'these are the aeroplanes now flying…' She (the Paris plane) taxies to her landing place. The mechanics run to her. The pilot heaves himself up in his seat, raises his goggles and steps out in a belted leather coat, groping for a cigarette. Men run up the steps…

This was 1926. A list of do's and dont's for cadets which is in the Heathrow visitors' centre forbids the wearing of spurs in the cockpit and enjoins the carrying of a handkerchief in order to wipe the goggles occasionally.

The second invasion was of sewage.
Carrying on the tradition of taking in London's
manure, sludge from sewage separated at
Isleworth was pumped seven miles for disposal
at the Perry Oaks Works on the west of
Heathrow.

During the war Heathrow was on the wrong
side of London to get heavily involved. Anyway
the RAF had Northolt. It was not until 1943
that the government proposed developing
Heathrow. It was, they said, in anticipation of a
distant war with Japan and a need for long-
range transport. Their motives were ques-
tioned by residents who saw their hamlets
including 28 listed buildings bulldozed to the
ground. This was done under the Defence of
the Realm Act (1939) from which there was no
appeal. There would be no public enquiry
unless the sewage works were involved. They
weren't. When Terminal 5 was proposed the
sewage works were again a rallying cry for the
opposition, this time because of their value as a
nature reserve. Eventually the authorities did

pay to create bird-friendly areas, but this last act in a 60 year old drama represented the final triumph of the airfield.

Also necessary for building T5 was the diversion of the two artificial rivers that run round the western and southern sides of Heathrow, known variously as the Duke of Northumberland's River, Longford, King's Cut or Queen's Cut. One had been built built by Henry VII to power mills at Isleworth, the other by Henry VIII to fill the fountains at Hampton Court.

Close by J13 the rivers Wraysbury, Colne and Thames come together. The Wraysbury is remarkable in that it appears in the centre of the roundabout at J13, travels a few yards and disappears again. However it is the larger river Colne, running through its valley to the east of the M25, that dictates the route of the motorway round to J22. This river valley, as with the Darenth by J3, has been much improved in recent times by the interest of the local authority in landscaping the area and opening up footpaths etc. for recreational use. The benefits are seen from the M25 after J14, where waste land has been cleared and planted.

The large town west of the M25 after J15 is Slough. In 1792 Archibald Robertson described it as

a large village in the (Bath) road about a mile and a half distant from Windsor, composed chiefly of one street, the houses are tolerably built and it contains some good inns.

Sir William Herschel put Slough on the map by setting up there his 40 foot telescope with a magnifying power of 6,000x; he chose Slough because the air was clear and there were few vibrations, both reasons seeming at the present day ironic. On the first night after he installed it, Herschel discovered two of Saturn's moons. ✿

Stained glass window at Herschel's parish church, St Laurence's, Upton, Slough, made by Andrew Taylor in 2000. It is based on Psalm 8: 'When I consider the heavens, the work of your fingers, the moon and the stars which you have set in their courses, what are mortals that you should be mindful of them?" .

When I consider the heavens, the work of your fingers, the Moon and stars which you have set in their courses, what are mortals that you should be mindful of them . . .

Psalm 8: 3–5.

Slough's leap into the 20th century came with the Great War. General Sir John Cowans, quartermaster of the army, was required to have ready fleets of motorised vehicles in the event of a rapid advance into Germany. The centre for this mechanised transport was established in Slough. However the sudden collapse of Germany in 1918 made these vehicles redundant. They were parked all over the area, many even on Kempton Park racecourse. Not surprisingly, the landowners wanted them removed. Slough was made the centre for the preparation and sale of the vehicles. Thereafter the empty sheds of the town were used as what is now termed an industrial estate for the production of margarine, plastics, biscuits, and cosmetics. The one-street village was no more. Betjeman famously wrote:

Come friendly bombs and fall on Slough
It isn't fit for humans now,
There isn't grass to graze a cow,
Swarm over, Death!

Pinewood Studios, with the motorway in the distance

The last bridge over the M25 before J16 leads to the Pinewood film studios (proud home of Carry On and James Bond), almost adjacent to the motorway, but invisible.✿ A more longstanding attraction is Burnham Beeches, a relic of medieval tree cover still maintained with the ancient pollarding techniques:

They are thus wanting in the feathery grace and sweep which form the characteristic beauty of the beech; but in exchange for this, the gnarled, twisted brances are in the very highest degree picturesque, and to the wearied Londoner few ways of spending a summer's day can be more enjoyable than a ramble over Burnham Knoll, with its turfy slopes and shaded dells, or better still, a picnic with some chosen friends in the shadow of one or other of these stupendous trees.

as the Revs. Manning and Green wrote in 1877.

Burnham Beechs from Manning and Green's English Pictures Drawn with Pen and Pencil

Clay Hills and the Colne Valley
J16 to J22

AFTER ONE MILE THE M25 runs under the A40 at Tatling End where a fire brigade practice tower is prominent south-side. Descending the slope one sees a blue-brick railway viaduct carrying trains over

Description
J16-J22

the motorway and the river Misbourne. There is farmland north, fencing south which gives way to views over the valley to Harefield. After 4 miles the county sign of Hertfordshire. From J17 to J18 is barely a mile. More farmland clockwise, and a view of the valley south. There is a viaduct over the Amersham railway and a steep climb between cuttings to J18.

Between J18 and J20 the journey is almost entirely within cuttings or obscured by embankments. The only view is that straight ahead of the Gade Viaduct at J20. This viaduct with its wide and unsightly concrete copings takes the M25 over the river Gade, the Grand Union Canal and a railway. North is Kings Langley, south Abbotts Langley. A former pig

Previous page: rural scene beneath the Gade Viaduct

The M25 looking west, Abbotts Langley top left. The former Ovaltine egg farm, later a pig farm, is at the bottom right, at the end of Egg Farm Lane

farm is prominent on the hillside north; it now houses a renewables company, signalled by a wind-turbine. The motorway then splits into two at different levels. Views of open country north, Watford south, before the M25 goes under the M1. Between J21A and J22 the tower of the former mental institution at Shenley is visible south. Two railways and the A5 then go over. North is the water tower of a Victorian hospital at Napsbury. Then northside the pseudo-Tudor buildings of a pastoral centre with its chapel. The river Colne is passed soon after the second railway bridge.

After J16 the road rises and, with the Colne Valley lying to the south and east, there is a feeling of driving over high ground throughout this section. But all is relative – at 328 feet (100 m) above sea level this section is only half the height of Reigate Hill (J8)!

THE BLUE-BRICK VIADUCT was built to carry the railway over the River Misbourne. Another, very simi-lar one can be seen a bit fur-ther north. Rather than impose a completely new solution, the road engineers

Construction
J16-J22

The Misbourne runs through its new tunnel. This view is the backdrop for BBC South East News

chose to run the **Misbourne** through a side arch and use both central arches for the **M25**. I suspect neither the French nor the Italians would have done it this way but it's something you might like to argue about. J19 is odd in that a spur road runs off towards Watford, signed and counted as part of the M25.

The Gade Valley Viaduct at 480 yards is the

largest bridge on the motorway, barring the Dartford Crossing itself. It consists of eleven spans of 138 feet (42 m) each with concrete Y-shaped supports set at an angle of 20 degrees so as not to obstruct the view of people in the valley below. For some reason these supports have not been spray-painted as those at New Haw (J11, p. 162).

Gade Valley Viaduct under construction

At J21/21A, with the M1 already in use, it was decided to run the M25 underneath it and site the link roads so as to minimise the environmental impact. In the end 130,000 shrubs and trees were planted here. Yet again this junction illustrates a failure to impose an overriding logic on the M25. An exasperated American I met at a party told me he had once left the M25 here, thinking he was well on his way to Manchester, only to find himself back in London. 'Whoever's heard of a junction 21A on a motor-way?' he fumed.

After J21A the contractors came across three old gravel workings that had subsequently been filled with rub-bish. Two, being dry, were easily cleared but the third was flooded. It was decided to deal with this by

The confusing J21A (top), and J21. The M25 runs top to bottom, underneath the M1

'dynamic compaction'. This meant dropping a weight of 16 tons from a height of 50 feet onto the rubbish until a solid mass was formed. Rubbish equal to 4.5 million domestic dustbins was by this means buried and sealed in.

J22 is significant as a high point that forms a watershed. A drop of rainwater falling west of J22 runs down via the Chess, Gade or Colne down to the Thames near Staines (J13), but a drop falling a few yards east will run down eventually into the River Lea which we meet later at J26 and which enters the Thames much lower down, near Canary Wharf.

EAST AND SOUTH OF THE M25 between J13 and J22 lies the Colne Valley with its two large towns of Rickmansworth and Watford. Beside the River Colne runs the Grand Union Canal, which did much a few centuries ago to develop the area. The canal

Background
J16-J22

Grand Union Canal

dated from an Act of Parliament of 1793 (later than the Wey Navigation at J10, 1651, and the Lea Navigation at J26, 1780, but destined to be the longest of all). It started as the Oxford Canal leading to the Thames at Brentford. In the following year a further section took it from Warwick to Birmingham and the whole became the Grand Union in 1805. Boats using it were normally 7 foot wide and 70 long.

Batchworth Lock next to the roundabout and bridge in lower Rickmansworth is ideal for an exploration of the area. It has a restaurant beside the canal, beautiful towpath walks, and a tour boat leaving hourly.

Alternatively one can find river and canal behind the lovely old village of Denham, which has all been set up for visitors. Information, tea and toilets may all be welcome but do they have to spoil it with a Pay and Display meter? North of the M25 are further picturesque villages: the Chalfonts, particularly Chalfont St Giles with Milton's Cottage, where he finished *Paradise Lost*. ✿

Immediately north of J17 there can be seen a narrow road leading from the roundabout into woodland. It is signposted Heronsgate. Here was the original settlement of the Chartist or National Land Co. in 1845. The company was founded by Feargus O'Connor a maverick leader of the Chartist movement. At a time when the working man and family, living in a rented house, owned little more than the clothes on their backs, it was O'Connor's idea that if sufficient workers could be got together, a few might be able to purchase land and live a healthy independent life on smallholdings.

> Where the cornland's pleasant tillage,
> Over waves the graceful hill
> And a wood embosn'd village
> Rises at O'Connorville.

All interested workers were invited to buy shares in the company, thereby generating the necessary fund and from those workers a few were to be chosen through a lottery to be the lucky recipients of the smallholdings at one of three sites around the country, the first being Heronsgate. There was also a political dimension which disturbed the establishment. One had at that time to have property worth 40 shillings a year to be eligible to vote. The smallholders would, therefore, become voters. Also, from the modest return they were required to make to the fund, further lotteries

Chartist cottage at Charterville in Oxfordshire, as it was built in its two acres of land. The ones at Heronsgate were virtually identical, but have mostly been altered

would be held and further smallholdings set up. The excitement of the lottery, the idealism of the first winners and the building of the first smallholdings all became national news. The government were concerned. Already they were looking suspiciously at the beginnings of the co-operative movement which, by banding workers together, looked like a nascent revolution. On the continent revolution was widespread in 1848. Parliament appointed a select committee to examine the scheme and in July 1848 it was declared illegal due to the lottery element in its workings. In 1851 a Winding-up Act was passed, in 1857 the estate was auctioned off, and in 1858 O'Connor died, a broken man. The narrow road one sees from the M25 runs for one mile and a half, 9 foot wide, into a land once filled with activity and hope. There are sad ghosts at J17.

J18 is the turning for Rickmansworth, where the rivers Chess, Gade and Colne flow together. Within a stone's throw of the motorway is the area associated with William Penn, a name writ large on a leisure centre and housing estate. Born in 1644, the son of a naval captain, he was imprisoned in 1670 for preaching to Quakers. Enduring the ups and downs of a dissenting leader in those times, he married and lived in Basing House, adjacent to Rickmansworth library, which is now kept as a museum.✿ For Americans, of course, he put the Penn into Pennsylvania. He is buried in the grounds of Jordans, an early Quaker meeting house nearby, which is still in use.✿

Over the river is Moor Park. Follow the narrow winding road through the park, now a golf club, and suddenly, dramatically, appears beside you the great bulk of the house.✿ This place was owned by the Archbishop of York (1460), by Cardinal Wolsey (1570), who lived in the valley, by the Earl of Bedford, the Duke of Ormonde and eventually, in 1670 the Duke of Monmouth.

Moor Park: the grand portico

Monmouth was James Fitzroy, an illegitimate son of Charles II. There was a slight chance that if he could legitimise his birth, he might succeed to the throne. Handsome and popular, he could not wait. He became involved with the Rye House Plot (of which more at J25) to assassinate Charles and his brother as they returned from Newmarket races. The plot was given away and the conspirators arrested. Monmouth begged mercy from Charles. His life spared, he was sent into exile. Two years later he landed in the West Country with a small army. Defeated at the first engagement, he was found hiding in a ditch, dressed as a labourer. The rebellion ended with Judge Jeffries and his bloody assizes. Monmouth again begged his father for mercy but this time was beheaded. Evelyn writes:

He would make no use of cap or other circum-stance but lying down bid the fellow do his office better than to my late Lord Russel and gave him gold: but the wretch made five chops before he had his head off which so incens'd the people that hade he not been guarded and got away they would have torn him to pieces… Thus ended this quondam Duke, darling of his father and the Ladys, being extraordinarily handsome and adroit, an excellent souldier and dauncer, a favorite of the people.

Nothing of Monmouth's house survives to the naked eye, it having been encased in a grand porticoed front by the next owner, a South Sea Bubble profiteer. The architect was long thought to be the Venetian Giacomo Leoni, and the interiors are grandiosely Italianate. More nouveaux riches followed, one of whom had the park transformed by Capability Brown – not for once necessarily a good thing, as they replaced

the perfectest figure of a garden I ever saw

in the words of Sir William Temple, who was so overwhelmed he even named his own house (near Farnham) Moor Park. And a final nouveau riche, Lord Leverhulme, turned the park into a golf course.

The M25 is now circling Watford (J19). It has been suggested that the 'Wat' may have been a person or may have meant simply 'wet'. Being on the canal between London and Aylesbury, Watford was a prosperous trading town, particularly known for brewing and wool. Its

Moor Park: one of the grand doorcases

later growth was due to the railways, as the census figures show — 3,530 in 1801; 29,327 in 1901; 56,799 in 1931. The great house here was Cassiobury Park. At first the property of the Abbots of St Albans, it was given by Henry VIII to Sir Richard Morison, a diplomat and one of the King's commissioners charged with enforcing the reformation at Oxford. His grand-daughter inherited the house and married the son of Sir Arthur Capel, whose own estate we encounter next to J25. A staunch royalist, Sir Arthur was executed by Cromwell in the Tower. His son, also Arthur Capel, having governed Ireland, was created Earl of Essex in 1661. John Evelyn visited him in these good days (1680):

The next day, upon the earnest invitation of the Earle of Essex went with him to his house of Cassioberie in Hartfordshire. It was on Sunday but going early from his Lordship's house in the Square of St Jamess we arrived by 10 o'clock. The house is new, a plaine fabric... there are in it divers faire and good rooms... when the hall is finished as his

Lordship designs it, together with the other wing, it will be a very noble palace… No man has been more industrious than this noble Lord in Planting about his seate, adorn'd with walkes, Ponds and other rural Elegancies but the soil is stonie, churlish and uneven nor is there water neere enough to the house though a very swift and cleare streame run within a flightshot from it in the valley.

Like Monmouth, Essex was implicated in the Rye House plot, although nothing was proven. With Lord Russell he was imprisoned in the Tower, in fact in the very same room occupied by his father before his execution 35 years earlier. It was all too much. Evelyn again:

As I was visiting Sir Tho Yarbrow and Lady in Covent Garden, that astonishing news of the Earle of Essex having cut his own Throate was brought to us, having now been but three dayes prisoner in the Tower and this happening on the very day and instant that the Lord Russel was on his trial and had sentence of death.

Charles II knew what Arthur Capel senior

had endured for the royal family. On being told the news he said

My Lord Essex might have tried my mercy; I owe a life to his family.

The last house at Cassiobury was built by the fifth Earl between 1800 and 1805, but was entirely demolished in 1927. The park (now public) with the river running through it, is, whatever Evelyn's opinion, a beautiful place.

North and south of J20 are Kings Langley and Abbotts Langley respectively. The king owned the first, the abbots of St Albans the second. At Kings Langley is the site of another royal palace long disappeared. In 1276 Eleanor of Castille lived here and in 1327 Edward III ruled from here during the Black Death. In 1431 the palace was badly damaged by fire –

through the negligence and drowsiness of a minstrel and insufficient care of a candle.

Canal by Abbotts Langley

Although granted by Henry VIII to three of his wives, not one of them lived there. Recent excavations have found only fragments of walls and a wine cellar.

Abbot's Langley was the native town of the only Englishman ever to become Pope; Nicholas Breakspear, who ruled as Adrian IV. Fuller, in his *Worthies*, writes

> He held his place four years, eight months and eight and twenty days; and in 1158, as he was drinking, was choked wth a fly; which in the large territory of St Peter's patrimony had no place but his throat to get into.

Just past J20 is a hillside that until recently was covered with pigs and their small detached residences. This is marked on the Ordnance Survey as the 'Ovaltine Egg Farm'. The Ovaltine factory itself, a large 1930's building can be seen from the M25 in the centre of Kings Langley. The three farms which produced milk and eggs for the factory were sold long ago. The buildings, having been suitably developed, have since February 2003 been the head office of Renewable Energy Systems, formerly of St Albans. Not only is there the unmissable wind-driven generator but also banks of solar cells. Meanwhile production of Ovaltine has moved to Switzerland and the factory may be demolished for residential development.

Wind turbine

The A5 crossing the motorway midway between J21A and J22 is the Roman Watling Street again, last seen near J2 but here running dead straight through the Edgware Road from London to St Albans, Cassivellaunus' capital before it became Roman Verulamium. Cassivellaunus resisted Caesar energetically in these marshy lands north of the Thames; Cassiobury may take its name from him

The Ovaltine Factory

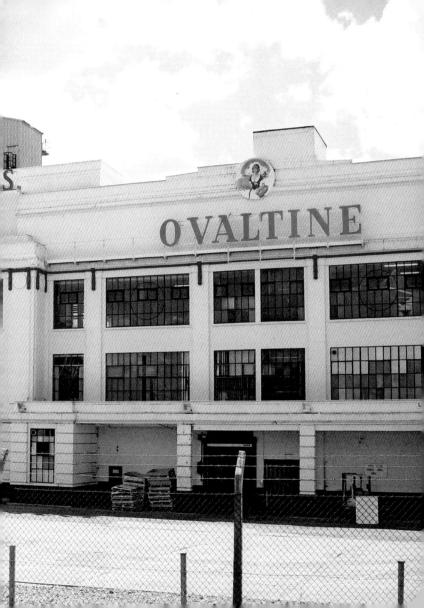

All Saints Pastoral Centre

Next, north of the M25 are the mock Tudor buildings of the **All Saints Pastoral Centre.** You can reckon on the general law that the nearer a building is to the motorway, the harder it is to find when you have left it, and this was no exception. But on telling the secretary that I was interested in the building I was amazed when she produced a printed booklet from a drawer and handed it to me. No need for pen and notebook. In the fields west of the present buildings are the ruins of a small chantry chapel last mentioned in 1566. The land was subsequently used for a large house, Colney House or Broad Colney, and the fields became parkland. This estate was sold in 1897 to the Society of All Saints Sisters of the Poor, a pioneering Anglican nursing order originally in the parish in Margaret St, W1, that had been a centre of the Oxford movement. About 200 sisters cared for the sick, the aged, and orphans. In 1899 the main building was rebuilt in a Tudor style and the chapel added in 1927. In 1973 the Sisters moved to Birmingham and the property was eventually taken over by the archbishopric of Westminster. The centre now provides courses and retreats for day and resident visitors

Just north of J22 is a very useful Savacentre within yards of the M25. It provides all the services of a motorway service area plus its shopping facility at half the cost. Beyond the Savacentre is the pretty village centre of London Colney with its stream, the last on our route to flow westward.

On to the Lea
J22 to J26

AFTER J22 THERE ARE VIEWS north and south; there are no more of the fences and screens that enclosed the motor-way between J9 and J16. The old coach road runs beside the M25 here, first on one side, then on the other. South is Salisbury Hall, a moated manor house sur-rounded by barns. Prominent ahead is the grain silo of Redwell Wood Farm. Shenley tower can be seen some two miles south. Finally the village of South Mimms appears straight ahead with its pub, the White Hart, at the foot of a triangle of buildings. The road crosses the Catherine Bourne and rises through cuttings to J23.

Description
J22-J26

If like me you tend to think of the M25 as a clockface, J23 (the A1, the road to the North) is 12.00. The Crossing is at 3.00 o'clock, Reigate at 6.00, the M4 at 9.00. This clockface is far from circular, the M25 varying between 23 miles and 12 miles from the centre of London,

Previous pages: South Mimms Services, J23

the centre being a moveable feast, shifting west as more bridges were built over the Thames.

After J23 there are farms north and south, and then before Potters Bar a school and sportsfield to the north. Once again the M25 splits into two halves at different levels. On both sides there is a row of concrete ventilation chimneys for a railway tunnel.

After J24 the water tower south is named Botany Bay. The tree-covered hill appearing as the forward horizon is Epping Forest. Trees both sides mark Enfield Chase. Blocks of flats in Enfield are visible south. Approaching J25 two important bridges go over. The first carries a road, the second, of metal, straight and square, carries a river! Finally, there is a railway bridge before the M25 enters the Holmesdale Tunnel.

After J25 there are four miles with factories on both sides. Epping Forest on the ridge dominates. Where pylons cross the motorway,

J25 from the air looking south: the motorway goes under the New River at the far right, and into the Holmesdale tunnel at the left

the **M25 bridges the River Lea and its canal, the Lea Navigation. A large area of ground south has been recently cleared for an industrial estate.**

THERE WERE FEW PROBLEMS with the junctions on this stretch. At J23 access to

South Mimms is a little awkward: the minor road leading to it seems to be in a lorry park outside the service area. But it was at South Mimms that Mrs. Thatcher officially opened the road, taking time to lambast those 'who carp and criticise'.

At J25 we come to the Holmesdale Tunnel. This was built to fulfil a guarantee given by planners to the builders and residents of the adjacent estates that they would not have to suffer the intrusion of a road with more than two lanes in each direction. The M25 had, therefore, at this point to disappear. An early plan for a high viaduct was rejected. The tunnel is 2,133 feet (650 m) long and cost almost £14 million. The walls required 883,000 cubic feet (25,000 cubic metres) of concrete and the roof was composed of 802 pre-cast beams, the largest of which weighs 39 tons. Information from 300 different positions within the tunnel is fed to a computer which records details of ventilation, lighting, drainage, fire protection and security. Drainage involves the use of pumps as the tunnel dips at the centre. Meanwhile the police at Chigwell view the tunnel via **CCTV** monitors.

AFTER J22 THE OLD COACH ROAD which runs beside the **M25** is of interest. It was designed by Thomas Telford for the government, which wanted to improve the time taken by mail coaches from that point to the centre of London – then,  incredibly, five hours. Most anxiously awaited (*c.* 1800) was news from Ireland, which came via Holyhead and the Great North Road. Telford's new road cut out South Mimms' High Street and the steep roads to the north where, it was said, a man could be washed off his feet by heavy rain. The White Hart, conspicuous from the M25, did not suffer, merely

Background J22-J26

transferring its sign from one side of the building to the other. Subsequently, Archway Road in north London was improved (with a more horse-friendly arch) in 1813, and then the Finchley Road in 1826, and the stage time was cut to one hour and forty minutes.

Salisbury Hall, seen on the old coach road to the south, is a moated manor house extended by Sir John Cuttes, Treasurer to Henry VIII. The barns behind the hall contain the Mosquito Aircraft Museum, where a staff of dedicated volunteers restore part or whole

Mosquito Aircraft Museum

Mosquitoes. They hope that lottery money might one day move them into more august premises.✿

Between J22 and J23 north of the motorway can be seen the buildings and tall tower of the former Shenley mental hospital. This has now been converted to residential use, but during the refurbishment I asked a builder whether they would demolish the tower. 'We daren't touch it,' he said, 'it's completely full of police electronics.'

South Mimms is in Domesday Book and at one time had a castle. In 1506 when the lord of the manor was Sir Roger Leukenor of Southmymhall, its population was 360, of whom a quarter were to die of plague. At that time Potters Bar was a hamlet of a dozen or so people at the entrance to Enfield Chase (hence the 'Bar'). So Potters Bar was dependent upon South Mimms, particularly for its church. The turnpike and eventually the railways were to transform this relationship. In 1835 Potters

Bar got its own chapel and in 1934, the ultimate indignity occurred – the Rural District of South Mimms became part of the Urban District of Potters Bar.

Enfield Chase was given to the de Mandeville family after the Norman Conquest. They lost it after Geoffrey de Mandeville, one more unfortunate Earl of Essex, was executed for treason in 1444. Incidentally, he was denied burial and his body hung for some years in an apple tree in the Temple. The Chase was royal under Elizabeth I and James I but Cromwell sold it off piecemeal. Once more, after the Restoration, it was 'afforested'. In 1676 Evelyn speaks of it as a lonely place:

Thence to Mr Secretary Coventries Lodge in the Chace which is a very pretty place, the house commodious, the Gardens handsome and our entertainment very free: there being none but my Lord and my selfe. That which I most admir'd at was, that in the compass of 25 miles (yet within 14 of London) there is never an house, barne, Church or building, besides three Lodges: To this Lodge there are three

greate ponds and some few enclosures, the rest a
solitarie desert, yet stored with no lesse than 3,006
deare etc. These are pretty retreates for Gent;
especially that were studious and a lover of privacy.

I found this place because of my wife who is
prone to get lost while driving. 'My mobile's
battery is gone,' she said. 'So I'm ringing you
from a hotel on the Cockfosters Road. This
looks a very nice place for tea. Where should I
be going?' I told her and we returned to the
South Park Hotel for tea – a portrait of Lord
Coventry on the wall, the name Evelyn on a
door. Not quite the same house – it was
rebuilt in 1836 – but very pleasant and two
miles south of J24. The Chase remained a forest until 1777 when it was finally disafforested.
In the meantime turnpike roads had arrived
and the area was more easily reached from
London. Many gentlemen were encouraged to
move there. Among them was General Byng
who built Wrotham Park, pronounced Rootam,
just south of the M25. The house may be
familiar under other names as it has been used

widely in films and television, most memorably in Altman's *Gosford Park*. In reality the present Mr. Byng relies on only four servants.

Wrotham, by the way, because his family came from that village in Kent. In 1756 the Admiral was leading a fleet to relieve Minorca, then besieged by the French, when he was

worsted in an initial action and decided to retire to Gibraltar. For this he was court-mar-tialled and shot for 'cowardice in the face of the enemy'. The execution brought from Voltaire the famous comment that the English like to shoot an admiral from time to time

Wrotham Park on the box

pour encourager les autres.

Byng's mansion is emphatically not open to the public but the fort in Minorca where the British were holed up apparently is. Lord John

Wrotham Park, or as much as can be seen by a member of the public from a footpath

Somers, Lord Chancellor under James II and William III, had also a country house here in Brookmans Park just north of Potters Bar, destroyed by fire in 1891.

At J25 another disappearing royal palace, Theobalds. A Dutch visitor, Constantine Huygens, mentioned it in the same breath as Windsor:

royal buildings as gigantic as the Pyramids and, rather than constituting a useless burden for the indignant earth, serving both as pleasure dwellings for great Kings and objects of pride and affection for British Gentlemen.

In fact it had not been royal to start with. The manor was bought by William Cecil, Lord Burghley, and in 1585 he built there a new house quickly famous for its opulence – two courtyards with four towers, each with four turrets surmounted by a gilded lion holding a weather vane. Formal gardens crossed by canals on which floated pleasure boats. Elizabeth I visited the house no fewer than fifteen times with her entourage, which must have been exceedingly expensive for her host. On the queen's death, James I travelled slowly from Edinburgh to London, his last stop being Theobalds. So impressed was he that he entertained the king

James I hunting: he is being presented with part of the deer.

of Denmark there in 1606 and in the next year asked Cecil to swap the house with him for Hatfield House. James enlarged Theobalds to 687 acres and put a brick wall $9\frac{1}{2}$ miles long round the park; he was a keen huntsman though unsteady on a horse.

Part of the entertainment for the king of Denmark was a masque presented by Ben Jonson. The Queen of Sheba tripped up into the royal guest's lap; the King tried to dance with her, but fell over drunk and had to be carried away; of the three virtues only Charity was sober enough to reach the royal presence:

she then returned to Hope and Faith, who were both sick in the lower hall.

James died at Theobalds, of a surfeit of fruit. Charles I was immediately proclaimed in the courtyard by a knight marshal who, instead of styling him 'rightful and indubitable heir' ominously used the words 'rightful and dubitable.' In later life Charles rarely went to Theobalds.

After Cromwell took over came the Parliament Act of 1649:

All honours, manors, castles, houses, messuages, chases, parks and land belonging to the late king Charles should be surveyed, valued, and sold for the benefit of the Commonwealth.

Theobalds was valued at £200 a year to rent; £8,275 11s. for sale as building materials. It was broken up. (Parts were incorporated into a nearby building, Old Palace House, bought by the council in 1965 but burnt down soon after.) As the county archivist writes:

thus within the span of 90 years the second largest building in England and the largest deer park were created and destroyed.

The estate passed through various hands, including those of another Oliver Cromwell, and in 1762 a third house was built by George Prescott MP, called Theobalds Park. In 1820 this was leased to Sir Henry Meux, the London brewer, whose wife wished to impress visitors

Temple Bar being prepared for its removal

with a superior entrance. She was told of
Temple Bar. This large stone structure
designed by Wren had stood in the Strand to
mark the limit of City jurisdiction until it was
taken down as an obstruction to traffic and was
lying in a scrap dealer's yard. This Lady Meux
bought and had erected as her park gate where
until very recently it still stood, damp and
desolate, among the trees a few yards from the
M25. It has now being moved yet again, to be

re-erected in London in the revamped precincts of St Paul's – two Wren buildings together. Theobalds House became a school, later a 'centre of excellence' of a building society, and is now a conference centre. The narrow road bridge just before J25, incidentally a Roman road, leads to it.

The New River which crosses on the boxed metal bridge just before J25 is not unconnected with Theobalds. It was noted at J13 that a scheme to take water from the Colne to London in the 17th century was abandoned; a

The Waterhouse in Islington, distribution point for New River waters, in the 17th century

similar scheme to use the River Lea was proposed by Edward Colthurst in 1600. In 1606 was passed 'An Acte for the Bringing in a freshe streame of Running Water to the Northe parts of the City of London'. It is no great distance from this area to the City, as may be appreciated from the Enfield road running south from J24, which has a surprisingly close view of the Thames as far as Greenwich. However, the water was to come from Hertford, 24 miles in a straight line but, following the 100 foot contour line as necessary, 40 miles. This would allow a total drop of 18 foot over the distance, or $5\frac{1}{2}$ inches

The New River today. Overleaf: the river is about to cross the motorway

per mile. The ditch was to be 10 foot wide and 4 deep, lined with clay. As Colthurst did not have sufficient money, the project was taken over by a City banker, Middleton. When digging was obstructed by landowners in 1610, the City appealed to the Privy Council, which ordered:

that all lette and hindrance may be removed and way given to Mr Middleton.

When the ditch approached His Majesty's land at Theobalds he offered it free passage and undertook half the costs – in return for half the profits. James is recorded as having been thrown into a frozen New River by his horse:

his attendants had to empty him, like an inverted cask, of the river-water he had drunk so freely against his will.

Only at one point did the New River cross a valley. It did so in a 666 foot lead trough on a timber frame 24 foot from the ground. Eventually it reached its distribution point close to Sadlers Wells. In 1613 the River was opened by the Lord Mayor and 175 houses were supplied via elm and lead pipes. Obviously this supply was appreciated: in 1708 Lady Wentworth is thinking of buying a house from Lord Sunderland in 'St Jamisis Squair' —

He asurse me none of the chimneys smoke and thear is New River water in all the offisis.

By 1834 there were 73,212 customers, and the river still delivers 38 million gallons per day to London. It can be seen by turning off south from J25, keeping to the outside lane and turning immediately right again.

Adjacent to the M25 and New River south-side is Capel Manor College. Originally the manor of Honeylands and Petriches, the estate came to be called more conveniently after its owners, the Capels. Sir William Capel, another Lord Mayor of London, acquired it in 1486. The subsequent unhappy story of this family has been told at J19 (see p. 214).

Capel Manor

The present house was built in the 1750's, its walled garden in 1786. Since 1968 it has been a horticultural college with exhibition gardens open to the public. Clydesdale horses are kept in the old stables and there is a haha in front of the house. ✿

   Turning north to Hoddesdon one finds the notorious **Rye House** signposted. ✿ Though only the gatehouse remains, this was one of the earliest brick buildings in the country, dating from 1443. It was here that the plot was hatched and from here that the conspirators set out to assassinate Charles II and his brother. The owner, Richard Rumbold, had served in Cromwell's army and took more of the blame, perhaps, than he should. The plot

Rye House

envisaged two dozen conspirators attacking the king and his Lifeguards. When all was discovered, Rumbold escaped from **Rye House** to the continent. He returned to raise a rebellion in Scotland as Monmouth landed in the south west. Wounded and taken prisoner, it was believed he would die within hours. Macaulay:

He was hastily tried, convicted and sentenced to be hanged and quartered within a few hours near the City Cross in the High Street (Edinburgh). Though unable to stand without the support of two men, he maintained his fortitude to the last and under the gibbet raised his feeble voice against popery and tyranny with such vehemence that the officers ordered the drums to strike up lest the people should hear him.

His head was placed on the West Port.

Halfway between Potters Bar and J24 north-side, about one mile distant, is the village of Cuffley, famous in the Great War for the shooting down of the first German airship by a 21-year old pilot, Lt William Leefe Robinson in 1916. The incident has in the light of greater events been largely forgotten, but at the time it was estimated that 60,000 people converged on Cuffley to view the wreckage. The pilot was awarded the VC. Captured after a forced landing in France, he survived the war but died in the great Asian flu epidemic of 1918.

Between J25 and J26 is the River Lea, and its canal, the Lea Navigation. The Lea runs in almost a straight line from Hertford down to Barking, where it joins the Thames close to Canary Wharf. For six hundred years its history was one of continuous aggravation. Essentially too many people were trying to use the same stretch of water for their own varying purposes. At Barking there was a monastery which had rights in land abutting the stream and where nets were spread to catch fish, a vital part of the monks' diet. This conflicted with the interests of the corn merchants sending their boats down river. Various water mills also lined the banks. To generate sufficient head of water they constructed weirs across the river.

The first legal wrangle concerning the tolls charged on boats dates from 1207. In 1275 the boatmen complained of being impeded by the weirs. In the 14th century a man from

The Lea Navigation

Chingford put piles and hurdles in ten places for the catching of fish, and the Abbot of Waltham did the same. Court cases followed. The weirs had only a simple central door through which boats might pass; once opened most of the water was lost. The millers refused to open them. In 1560 two Dutchmen were asked to study the problem and in 1577 the first mitre gated lock was built at Waltham. As river transport improved, it was the turn of the waggoners to become worried.

Barges were taking two days down to the Thames and four hours up to the City: waggons took a week. The bargemen called the waggoners

idle loitering careless people as they are which do nothing but ride ten miles a day upon a sack, pestering the highways.

By 1581 the waggoners were on the attack; river banks were knocked in, Waltham lock set on fire, and trees felled across the river. The

The Lea

bargemen were attacked with staves, swords and daggers; men and cargoes were thrown into the river. However during the great plague the bargemen continued to supply the City and were rewarded with the Freedom of the Thames. Similarly in 1667 during the Dutch Wars, with the coast unsafe, coal was brought by barge to Cambridge, loaded on packhorses to Ware and then brought down the Lea. But then the barges grounded – the New River was siphoning off water for drinking. Finally in 1766 a new canal was planned, was working and making a profit by 1780. It was the one seen today next to the river. At last everyone was happy. The River Lea was used for fish and drove the mills; the Lea Navigation was used by the boats, and drinking water came from the New River. Only the waggoners lost out; but they, of course, eventually bought lorries and took the trade from the canal.

The Lea Valley Park acts as does its sisters, the Colne and the Darenth, to make the area more accessible to the public. There is a visitors' centre, well-signposted, at Waltham just north of J26.✿ There is understandable confusion between Waltham Abbey with its church of the Holy Cross, named after a relic, and Waltham Cross which got its name, as did Charing Cross, from being one of the resting places for the body of Eleanor of Castile on its journey south. Affixed to the railings around

Eleanor Cross with replacement statues in Waltham Cross

Waltham Cross is a small sign which states that the figures of Edward I and Queen Eleanor are copies, and that the originals have been removed for their conservation to the library in Hertford. Interested both to see the medieval art and satisfy my curiosity about this marriage of 36 years which began, like most, as a political arrangement but obviously became much more than that, I set off to Hertford the very next day. It was a journey of some 50 miles and ended with the customary difficulties of locating the library and parking the car. I entered the library and cheerfully informed the young couple behind the counter that I had come to see Edward I. They looked at a total loss. My eyes wandered round the shelves, hopeful of seeing the royal statues. An older lady who had been sitting at a desk with her back to me turned round. 'Oh dear', she said,

we have about one person every year coming here to see the statues of Edward I and Queen Eleanor. I am afraid they were moved to the Victoria and

Albert Museum about fifteen years ago. I do wish the Council would change that sign.

Waltham Abbey's royal history goes back further, since Harold and his wife Edith of the Swan Neck are supposed to be buried under the altar; the Abbey's current buildings are rather later, since it was one of three founded by Henry II to expiate the murder of Becket. It was also the last of the monasteries to be destroyed by Henry VIII, its church being spared. A brass rod in the Abbey grounds marks the position of the Greenwich Meridian. The peal is Tennyson's 'Ring out, wild bells!'; he was hard at work on *In Memoriam* at Epping.

Waltham Abbey

Waltham Abbey: the Cattle Market between the wars

Cattle Market Waltham Abbey.

About 1600 production of gunpowder began in Waltham. It was one of the highlights of Essex, according to Fuller's *Worthies*:

More [powders] are made by mills of late erected on the river Ley, betwixt Waltham and London, than in all England besides... It consisteth of three essential ingredients.
1. Brimstone, whose office is to catch fire and flame of a sudden, and convey it to the other two.
2. Charcoal pulverized, which continueth the fire, and quencheth the flame, which otherwise would consume the strength thereof.
3. Saltpetre, which causeth a windy exhalation, and driveth forth the bullet.
The gunpowder is the emblem of politic revenge, for it biteth first and barketh afterwards, the bullet being at the mark before the report is heard, so that it maketh a noise, not by way of warning, but triumph.

Eventually the powder mills grew into an arms industry including rifles and machine guns. It was then realised, as with the Arsenal at Woolwich that, handy though it might be for

the munitions worker to have the factory at the end of his road, it engendered a certain amount of risk. In 1890 the Royal Gunpowder Factory was moved to the vast site adjacent to the Lea and now the motorway. In 1914 this factory was the sole supplier to the British army of guncotton and became the economic mainstay of the town. Production ceased in 1943 and until recently the site was used as a defence research establishment. Now cleared, it will be an industrial park and housing estate.

Some 400 acres in the north of the site have been taken over by a trust to establish it as a visitor attraction, known as the Royal Gunpowder Mills. This enormous area can only be covered on their land train and in fact without the commentary they give the site is almost impossible to comprehend. All credit to the band of volunteers who have got this project off the ground and are determined to make a success of it.✿

Back to the Crossing
Crossing
J26 to J31

AFTER J26 THE M25 climbs to Epping Forest with a crawler lane – the only one on the whole motorway. The roofless mansion of Copped Hall can just be seen north clockwise, prominent anti-clockwise. Then the Bell Common Tunnel is followed by the descent to J27, the M11 interchange. The views are of Epping north, Theydon Bois south.

Description J26-J31

Immediately after J27, on the summit of a hill to the north, is Hill Hall, red brick; to the south is Stapleford Airport. After three miles a large white building north with cedars of Lebanon, Sutton Place, dominates the valley to anti-clockwise traffic. The River Roding runs at the bottom of valley to the south. The hills with aerials far to the north are Kelvedon Hatch. The white water tower south is at Havering atte Bower – where it stands in a private garden.

Previous pages: Bell Common Tunnel from the air looking north, showing the cricket pitch

At J28 a farmhouse, **The Poplars**, a red-brick Victorian/Edwardian house, is clearly seen before the M25 enters a long cutting. You emerge to a view from the top over towards East London, and then the motorway descends to J29, the Southend road (A127). Already the power station at the river crossing can be seen.

From J29 anti-clockwise glimpses may be had of the Ford Company buildings on the hill you have just descended. Similarly, the moated medieval house west of the M25 is prominent only to anti-clockwise drivers. The original B road runnning north-south runs parallel with

Lakeside Shopping Centre, with the Crossing beyond

the motorway that replaced it, passing through the village of Ockendon. A large embankment east protects Kemps Farm. Several bridges over precede J30, the slip to Lakeside Shopping Centre. ✿

At J30 a river enclosed by concrete banks runs under the bridge at the centre of the junction; this is the Mar Dyke. Just after this west is the red brick Purfleet Hotel with Purfleet F.C.'s ground in front of it. As the road rises to the bridge, it is once more on chalk.

SMALL SCALE GEOLOGICAL MAPS show that the M25 has been on London Clay since J22, but a larger scale shows local deposits of sand, pebbles and mixed clays keeping the road from the clay beneath. After J28 the road enters a deep cutting through this clay. Without the building of any great interchange this section cost over

Construction J26-J31

£30 million, which indicates how heavy the work was.

At J26 the motorway contractors decided to move rather than destroy a small 18th century *cottage orné*, a kind of chalet bungalow with thatched roof, which stood in their way. Unfortunately the walls crumbled to pieces as soon as they were touched and the bits and pieces were put aside to be incorporated in a rebuild beside the motorway.

` The house at J26

The house now stands in a dip a few yards north of the M25. While I was examining it the lady of the house arrived home from shopping. 'Which bits are original?' I asked. 'Nothing,' she said.

Even the staircase was stolen while it lay ready for
the re-build.

So the house is there but it isn't, if you see
what I mean.

The Bell Common Tunnel comes next. It is
shorter than the Holmesdale (1,540 feet as
against 2,130, 470 m to 650 m) and has no dip
in it requiring drainage, pumping etc. This
tunnel was made necessary by the first rule of
all forests, and here Epping Forest, that there
should be no enclosure. If the M25 had to
bisect the forest then free movement had to be
provided between the parts. It so happened
that among the sports facilities provided within
the forest, a cricket pitch used by the Epping
Foresters C.C. (founded 1947), occupied the
precise spot the M25 was to cross. The club
was therefore found an alternative pitch during
the four years of construction and provided
with a new pavilion on their return. The pitch,
which is now quite literally on the M25, is
screened from it by scrub and small trees so

that from above one is quite unconscious of its unique position.

Apart from the stretches of embankment which keep the M25 above the Essex marshes, the main feature after J29 is the viaduct over the Mar Dyke, which cost £4 million more than the road leading to it. The final stretch of the M25 has been twice widened, once for the second tunnel in 1982 and then, most recently, for the bridge.

NORTH OF THE M25 on the stretch before the second tunnel, stark and imposing to anti-clockwise traffic, easily missed  by clockwise, is Copped Hall or Copthall, the name coming either from its standing on a ridge or having a ridged roof. The house merits only one line in Pevsner's *Buildings of England* but nevertheless the M25 is here running through the park of an historic estate.

Copped Hall

The original manor house stood slightly to the west of the present one. From 1350 to 1537 it belonged to Waltham Abbey. In 1548 Edward VI had Mary Tudor live here much as that lady had her half-sister live at Hatfield. Here in 1551 there was a fuss about Mary

taking the Catholic Mass. Elizabeth granted
the house to Thomas Heneage, a courtier. The
queen stayed there in 1568 and it seems that
as part of Heneage's wedding celebrations, *A
Midsummer Night's Dream* may have received its
first performance. In 1688 Princess Anne
stayed overnight at the hall during her escape.
This old building was replaced by the new in

Copped Hall : garden pavilion

1753 and this was again
greatly extended in the
1800's. The fire which
gutted the building
occurred in 1917. The
house had been roofless
for over seventy years
when the Copped Hall
Trust was established in
1993; they bought the
freehold of the Hall in

1995. (Some 600 acres of the park around the
Hall had been acquired by the Corporation of
the City of London in 1992.) In 1999 the trust
bought the walled garden, at four acres one of
the largest in England. We have within a very

short space already met the volunteers of the
aircraft museum (J22) and the restorers of the
Gunpowder Mills (J26), now we meet the
'Friends of Copped Hall', close on 400 in number, who 'raise funds, organise tours of the
grounds, visit groups to recount the history of
the house and assist the trust with other educational and social activities'. In particular
they meet (mainly on Sunday mornings) to do
the hard work of clearing the gardens and
moving masonry. With no vast sum of money
at their disposal the aims of the trust are
essentially defensive – secure the chimneys,
install a temporary girder roof, restore the
interior and deter vandalism. One can only
admire all these people and their efforts.✿

Beside and opposite Copped Hall runs
Epping Forest. In 1100 three quarters of Essex
is said to have been royal forest. By 1300 this
was down to 60,000 acres about Waltham,
including Epping. Enclosures continued: in
1851 Hainault was disafforested, the trees cut,
the land ploughed. Thereafter landowners in

Epping began to enclose. In 1871 the Corporation of London, owning some land in the forest, had, as commoners, the right to object to the enclosure and went to court. They won the case and proceeded to buy, in 1875, 13,500 acres of unused land within the forest. Two Acts of Parliament regularised the position in 1878; the Corporation were made Conservators of the Forest and were enabled to

acquire and safeguard land within 25 miles of the City for 'recreation and enjoyment'. Queen Victoria officially opened the forest in 1882.

Above, Queen Elizabeth 'hunting'. Opposite, the Queen's Standing

At the forest's southern tip is a relic of earlier royal attention, the Queen's Standing. This is a Tudor timbered building put up for Henry VIII and enjoyed by Elizabeth. There she could view the hunt and shoot any deer that came near enough, a procedure which is no

Nᵒ

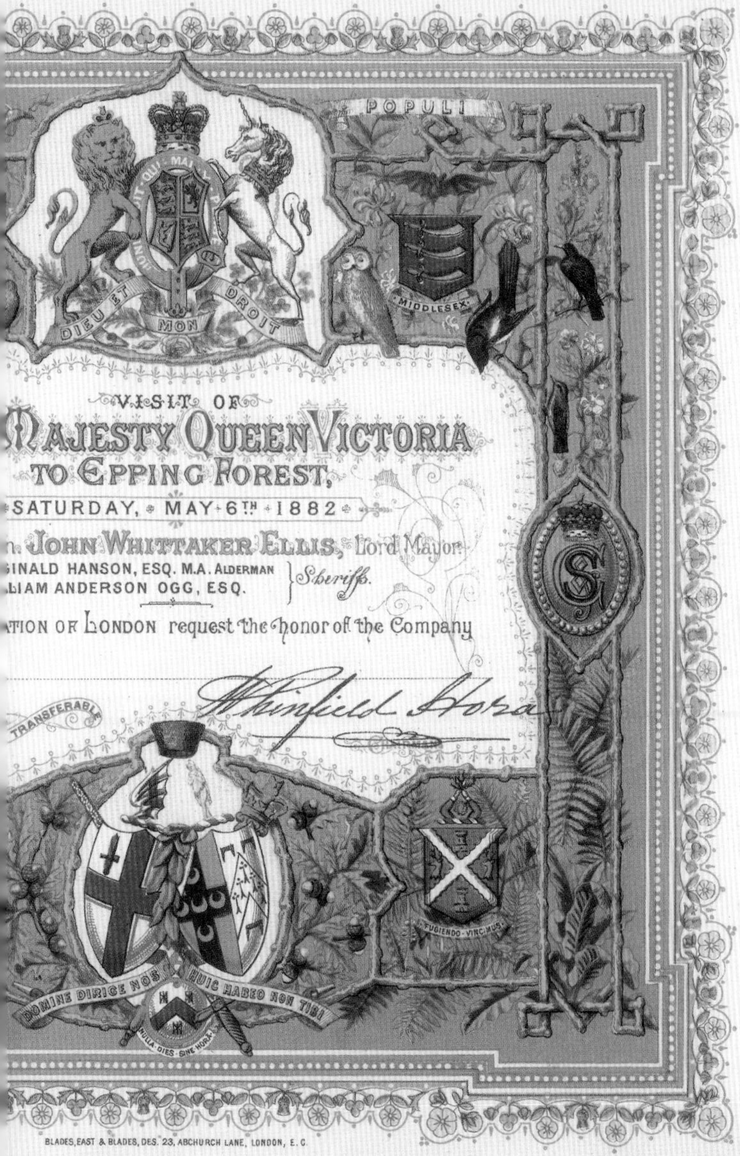

POPULI
DIEU ET MON DROIT
MIDDLESEX
VISIT OF
MAJESTY QUEEN VICTORIA
TO EPPING FOREST,
SATURDAY, MAY 6TH 1882
JOHN WHITTAKER ELLIS, Lord Mayor
GINALD HANSON, ESQ. M.A. ALDERMAN
LIAM ANDERSON OGG, ESQ.
Sheriffs.
ATION OF LONDON request the honor of the Company
TRANSFERABLE
DOMINE DIRIGE NOS
HUIC HABEO NON TIBI
NULLA DIES SINE HORA
FUGIENDO VINCIMUS
BLADES, EAST & BLADES, DES. 23, ABCHURCH LANE, LONDON, E.C.

doubt now 'wholly unacceptable.'✿

By the 20th century the deer were getting rarer. Between 1948 and 1958 numbers dropped from 182 to 63, owing, mostly, to road accidents. When trees were cut back to improve motorists' vision, the deer fed on the verges. Does were giving birth outside the forest boundary in Copped Hall and Theydon Bois. A buck and several does were sent to Whipsnade Zoo for protection. In 1960 a sanctuary was built at Birch Hall with a fence deer could jump but which kept dogs out. By 1970 numbers had recovered to 92. With a 20 mph speed limit and sleeping policemen, the deer are now plentiful.

The Corporation's efforts are not always popular. A local newspaper interviewed Bert Miller, 'who has a tea stall in the forest and blames the gradual deterioration of the forest on conservationists':

Previous pages: the official invitation to the opening of Epping Forest

They worry about thistles and stinging nettles for the butterflies. It's another word for filth as far as I'm concerned.

By contrast with the summary treatment of Copped Hall, Hill Hall, prominent on the summit of the hill just northeast of J27, gets two pages in Pevsner. It was built by Sir Thomas Smith between 1557 and 1570. A Cambridge scholar at 13, and thereafter a lecturer in Paris, Orleans and Padua, Sir Thomas became Secretary of State in 1547 and Ambassador

Hill Hall

to France in 1562. He therefore returned to England with a knowledge of continental architecture which shows in the Hall, the earliest structure in England to incorporate the classical elements which were to become so common. The Smith family lived at the Hall until 1923 when it was sold to a Mrs Hunter, known as a society hostess.

During WWII both soldiers and prisoners were billetted there. In 1952 it became a women's open prison whose most notorious inmate was Miss Christine Keeler. In 1969 it was gutted by fire; in the ensuing restoration Tudor wall paintings were discovered. Recently re-roofed by English Heritage, the house has been turned into flats, some with their own cinema rooms.✿

Past J27 southside and over the next hill is Stapleford Airport, opened in 1934 by Hillman's Airways to provide charter flights. Although they took a 25-year lease and built three hangars, two years later they moved to Heston. From 1938 to 1945 the RAF took over, basing several squadrons of Hurricanes there and working closely with the larger field at North Weald up the M11. Now it is the home of a private flying club, a flying school and of another charter company, **Stapleford Executive Airline.**

The **River Roding,** whose widening was 'promoted' by Act of Parliament in 1737 but not completed till 1764, wanders through this wide valley on its way south to join the Thames not far from the Lea. Canoeists relish it for the chance to wave at cars in traffic jams as they glide past, but in reality much of the Roding is slow work for them too, being little more than a glorified ditch. The village it runs to south of the M25 is **Abridge** where there is an old bridge, bullrushes and where the **Blue Boar** glowers over the road at the **White Hart.** In winter the Roding is a more respectable size and floods the fields by the bridge.

North of the M25, dominating the valley as seen by anti-clockwise drivers is **Suttons.** This large white building, with another to the left of it and a striped awning to the right, has

Overleaf: the bridge at Abridge. The motorway is two fields away

Orangery at Suttons

mystified many drivers. It was the manor house, 'the handsome and pleasant seat of Sir C. Smith Bart., the lord of the manor of Suttons' and you are driving across his fields. However Sir C. Smith is long gone and the house is now a private health clinic catering mainly for psychiatric patients. The smaller building was originally its orangery. Macaulay speaks of a nobleman 'retiring to his library, his orangery and his tulips.' This orangery is now separate and contains a swimming pool (dis-used). The awning leads to the patients' restaurant.

High on the ridge behind Suttons, at Kelvedon Hatch, marked only by an aerial, is a secret nuclear bunker. Built in 1952, this 3-storey underground shelter was to be used as the refuge for a skeleton administration in the event of nuclear war. Services within the bunker were designed to sustain 600 people for three

Innocuous exterior of the bunker

months. The rest of us were advised to hide under the stairs covered by mattresses.❀

Prominent at J28 on the east side is an Edwardian farmhouse called The Poplars. A plaque between the bedroom windows reads 'F. W. Harris 1906'. Mrs Kingston (*née* Harris)

The Poplars

tells me that this is misleading as the front was only the last of many extensions to a building that has been there for at least a century and a half. Both Mr and Mrs Kingston speak with bitterness of the M25 and three Ordnance Survey maps in Brentwood Library suggest why.

The map of 1961 shows a quiet country valley with only two roads. In a straight line along the valley floor runs the A12, a two-lane road built originally by the Romans to lead from

London via Chelmsford and Colchester to Caistor in Norfolk. The sides of the valley being too steep for traffic to be hauled across it, a lane runs from the Nag's Head public house obliquely across the back of the hillside to Upminster. Occasionally the yacking of tractors, the clipping of horses' hooves and the rumble of a lorry might have been drowned by the passing of a train on the hilltop one field distant above the Poplars. This line was built by the Eastern Counties Railway in 1843, so people were used to it.

A map of 1968 shows an enormous change. A very large roundabout has appeared outside the Poplars. 'The old road' as they call it locally, has been moved some 100 yards into the Poplars' frontage with its name changed to A1023, and a new dual carriageway, 'the bypass' is built to avoid Brentwood and inherit the name A12. Over the hill behind the Poplars, cutting its way through the clay which was formerly too steep, is shown, in dotted lines, the M25.

By 1974, the date of the third map, the
motorway has arrived. Beside the Poplars and
not 40 yards distant are two slip roads of two
lanes each and a motorway of six lanes. Over
38 acres of the
farm are on the
far side of the
M25. The authori-
ties maintain that
the provision of a
bridge or tunnel
across the ten
lanes of motorway
and slips would be

The Poplars and the M25

prohibitively expensive: the Kingstons must put
their animals in a motor vehicle and drive
them round the roundabout.

The noise is deafening. The three roads give
a total of 16 lanes of traffic near the house.
The A12 is signposted as 'an alternative route
to East Anglia'. Lorries are everywhere. Traffic
lights on the roundabout ensure Grand Prix
starts and screeching brakes. On only one day

a year are there no lorries and the Kingstons
are disorientated by the silence – Christmas
Day. Looking back to 1961, can you wonder
that they're bitter?

Another deer park adjacent to the motorway and well worth finding by a circuitous
route is Weald Hall. Take the A 1023 from J28
– take extreme care not to go on the A12 by
mistake – turn left up Wiggley Bush Lane to
Weald village from where the park is signposted. In 1848 'the little market town of
Brentwood' was in the parish of Weald but
with the coming of the railways, as at South
Mimms/Potters Bar, the offspring outgrew the
parent. Dating from 1540, Weald Hall and its
deer survived until WWII when the Hall was
damaged by fire, the deer escaped, and the
army threw unwanted ammunition into the
lake. In 1946 the Metropolitan Railway Estates
Company took over. They ploughed up the
land and demolished the Hall, whose contents
were auctioned for £1,000. The park has, since
1953, been restored by Essex County Council

and deer reintroduced. Food to be fed to the deer is available to young customers at the visitors' centre.❁

In fact the countryside north of J27 to J28 may be a surprise to those who only know the flat lands of the Essex marshes. This is an area of friendly lanes with clipped grass verges and disorganised villages.

It takes only a few minutes to drive from J28 to J29 where the last of the many hills on the northern route is left behind. Travelling anti-clockwise, on the summit of this final hill can be seen a tall office building, the headquarters of the Ford Motor Company in Warley. It needs a flash of sunlight to pick it out amongst the trees.

Prior to the building of the M25, traffic had to use the small country road lying under a mile to the east. Here were two great houses, Groves and Ockendon Hall, the latter

Deer from Weald Hall graze next to M25

Sir Richard Saltonstall, wife and family

destroyed by bombs in WWII. The former was the home of Sir Richard Saltonstall, whose wealth and lifestyle are reminiscent of Sir Robert Clayton (J6, p. 113). Saltonstall was a

merchant who financed 31 ships to face the
Armada. In 1597 he was Lord Mayor and he
too has an alabaster mon-
ument in the local church.

A mile after J29 west-
side is a house and out-
buildings prominent to
anti-clockwise traffic. It
has the appearance of a
wooden-framed Tudor
building with lath and
plaster walls. However,
the section beneath the
left-hand gable has been
missing for years and I
doubted the authenticity

Flint church at S. Ockendon

of the whole. At last a customer en route to
Stansted Airport asked me directly what it was
and I had to confess I did not know. On the
way back I made the necessary deviation and
found Tom restoring a piece of furniture in
one of the outhouses. 'It's genuine fifteenth
century,' he said:

But I've been to the Public Record Office in Chelmsford and can't tell you much more about it. Now Franks Farm, it may have been the Manor House of Franks. No-one knows. There could have been a family called Franks or it could have been named after a family from France. I can tell you, though, why the front is still missing off that gable. They had some craftsmen down from Lavenham in Suffolk to restore it but instead of sticking the plaster to chicken wire as most do, they used laths as used to be the custom. After they finished the plaster all fell off.

More successfully oak beams have been driven under the walls to stop the house sinking and a ditch has been cut around two sides to drain off water. Inside are two great inglenooks.

Midway between J29 and J30 eastside, within yards of the M25, trying to hide behind an earthen embankment raised by themselves, are the residents of Kemps Farm, a formerly peaceful farmstead with two fish ponds and a couple of cottages in the middle of nowhere.

Here, they tell me, noise is normally bad but doubly so in wet weather. Worst of all are traffic jams which cause the lorries to use their airbrakes. Some vibration from these sets the dogs barking.

Perhaps at this point one should say something about the large trucks that are such a feature of the motorway. On a Friday in February 2004, between 1300 and 1315 hours I counted 261 trucks passing the Dartford Crossing anti-clockwise and 170 going in the opposite direction, an hourly rate of 1,000 one way, 700 the other, numbers difficult to believe. However, those in the trade tell me that there are no more trucks registered now in Britain than there were in the 1950's, approximately 500,000. The main difference is one of size, the typical 50's truck of 150 HP pulled 24 tons; its modern counterpart with 430 HP pulls 44 tons. There are also of course the foreign trucks, Norbert Dentresangle and Willi Betz being as common as Eddie Stobart.

With those running only a short distance as, for example, the supermarket lorries delivering from their depots, Sainsbury's (J26), Tesco (J31) and Asda (J1a), there is no problem. The difficulty for the longer distance drivers is where to park their giants overnight. The three service areas on the M25 each take about 150 trucks and Truck World off J31 takes a further 250, the latter being completely full by 6.00 in the evening. The fourth promised service area on the M25 has never been

The sleeping giants set off at dawn

built and the police have denied trucks the use of the slip roads at Clackets. You cannot park these colossal machines just anywhere. One alternative is to find a layby down an A-road, and that is where you may find many of these sleeping giants overnight. I mention the matter only to point out to the car driver that the driver of the big truck has preoccupations he might not have guessed at.

Arriving at J30 with the concrete bridges circling above you, you might not notice the Mar Dyke below. Sometimes it is a dribble in its concrete ditch, sometimes a flood over the fields both sides. It was built to drain the Bulphan Fens, an area beyond the Ockendons with narrow roads and deep drainage ditches.

Mar Dyke sign
Overleaf, the Mar Dyke

The story is that local men had as many as ten or twelve wives. They married girls from the hilly country who, when they arrived in the fens succumbed to 'the ague', a mosquito-borne disease (perhaps malaria), so they were soon off to marry another one. The Mar Dyke also doubled as a transport system for the fen farmers to bring their produce to Aveley market. There was dispute about who should have first choice of this produce, locals or 'foreigners' from Kent. Eventually a first bell was rung to open the market to locals, a second to admit 'foreigners'. Lest you think this an exaggeration I can tell you that I asked an old Kentish countryman back in 1953 whether he had ever been abroad. 'Yes,' he said seriously.

One time I went over the water to Essex.

Close to J30, up the steep grass bank was Belhus Park, the home of John Barrett, a lawyer under Henry VIII. With the English aversion to foreign-sounding names the estate was never called 'Belhus', but always 'Barretts'.

It was described in 1809 thus:

> It has all the features of a baronial mansion, with
> battlements, turrets, and small windows of the
> structure which prevailed in the reign of Henry
> VIII… the apartments of the house are very magnif-
> icent and ornamented with stained glass… the park
> and grounds are extensive and well laid out by the
> genius of Capability Brown.

The house became derelict in 1956, needing an estimated £35,000 for repairs. It was demolished. Belhus Park is now a public open space containing parkland, a leisure centre, painted pink, and a golf course with driving

Belhus

range. It is the high netting of the latter which is so visible from the M25, together with the bridge (the last before J30/J31) that joins the two parts of the park divided by the motorway. ✿

After J30/J31 the road begins to rise again, once more climbing to the River Crossing. The familiar roofs appear below on both sides. Here are the 50 mph signs. It's time to rummage for a pound coin for the toll. The river is shining below. Driving in a circle you have been over or under every road, river, canal, railway, telegraph wire or water pipe that connects our capital city to the rest of the country. It's been a long journey; you have travelled 117 miles clockwise.

Chaos at J31. A lorry has left the M25 centre right and either its contents or foam can be seen spread out over the roundabout. Sand has been scattered over the motorway and traffic is diverted from top left to botom right.
A view we mortals rarely get.

THIS TABLET WAS
AFFIXED IN 1926 TO COMMEMORATE
THE 200TH ANNIVERSARY OF THE BIRTH OF
MAJOR GENERAL WILLIAM ROY F.R.S.
BORN 4TH MAY 1726 — DIED 1ST JULY 1790.
HE CONCEIVED THE IDEA OF CARRYING OUT THE TRIANGULATION
OF THE COUNTRY AND OF CONSTRUCTING A COMPLETE AND
ACCURATE MAP AND THEREBY LAID THE FOUNDATION OF THE
ORDNANCE SURVEY

THIS GUN MARKS THE N.W. TERMINUS OF THE BASE WHICH WAS MEASURED IN 1784
UNDER THE SUPERVISION OF GENERAL ROY AS PART OF THE OPERATIONS FOR
DETERMINING THE RELATIVE POSITIONS OF THE GREENWICH AND PARIS
OBSERVATORIES — THIS MEASUREMENT WAS RENDERED POSSIBLE BY THE
MUNIFICENCE OF H.M. KING GEORGE III WHO INSPECTED THE WORK ON 21ST AUGUST 1784.
THE BASE WAS MEASURED AGAIN IN 1791 BY CAPTAIN MUDGE AS THE COMMENCEMENT
OF THE PRINCIPAL TRIANGULATION OF
● — GREAT BRITAIN — ●
LENGTH OF BASE - REDUCED TO M.S.L.

	FEET
AS MEASURED BY ROY	27404·01 FEET
" " " GLUDGE	27404·24 "
AS DETERMINED BY CLARKE IN 1858 IN TERMS	27406·19 "
OF THE ORDNANCE SURVEY STANDARD O[1]	

p. 53 Crossness Sewage Works **Steamings several times a year; details from www.crossness.org.uk**

p. 65 Bluewater **Core trading: Mon-Fri 10-9, Sat 9-8, Sun 11-5, BH Mons. 10-6; www.bluewater.co.uk**

Opening Times

p. 72 Brands Hatch **Mon-Fri 7am-8 pm; events till half an hour after racing; www.motorsportvision.co.uk**

p. 76 Lullingstone Roman Villa **Apr-Sept: daily 10-6; Oct-Nov daily 10-4; Dec-Jan Wed-Sun 10-4; Feb-Mar daily 10-4; www. english-heritage. org.uk**

p. 76 Lullingstone Castle **Apr-Oct Fri & Sat 12-5, Sun 2-6; www.lullingstonecastle. co.uk**

p. 80 Eagle Heights **May-Oct 9.30-5.30. Demonstration flights at 12 and 1. Open in winter with shorter hours.**

p. 104 Squerryes **Wed, Sat Sun & Bank Hols, 1st April to 30th Sep, 1.30 to 5.30.**

p. 104 Quebec House **Apr-Oct Tues-Sun 2-5.30; www.national-trust.org.uk**

p. 104 Chartwell **End Mar-end June, Wed-Sun 11-5; Jul-end Aug, Tue-Sun 11-5, Sep-Nov, Wed-Sun 11-5; www.nationaltrust.org.uk**

p. 107 Titsey **May Bank Holiday and mid May-end Sep, Wed-Sun & BH Mon 1-5; www.titsey.com**

p. 116 Godstone Vineyard **May-end Sep, Mon-Fri, 10.30-4.30, Sat**

& Sun 10-5.30; Oct-end Apr, Mon-Fri, 11-4, Sat & Sun 10-4.30;
www.godstonevineyards.com

p. 119 Orpheus Trust **For courses call 01883 744644 or email
enquiries@orpheus.org.uk**

p. 125 Gravelly Hill **The tower is not open to the public.**

p. 135 Gatton **The headmaster regrets that his responsibilites
do not allow him to admit the public to any of the six historic
sites at Gatton.**

p. 151 Fire and Iron Gallery **Mon-Sat 10-5;
www.fireandiron.co.uk**

p. 155 Chatley Heath Semaphore Tower **Mon-Sat
10-5 summer, 10-4 winter**

p. 158 Painshill **Mar-Oct, Tues-Sun 10.30-6; Nov-Feb, Wed-Sun
11-4 or dusk; www.painshill.co.uk**

p. 158 Royal Horticultural Society Gardens, Wisley
**Mar-Oct, Mon-Fri 10-5, Sat & Sun 9-5; BH Mon 9-5 (time of last
admission; closes 1 hour later); Nov-Feb, Mon-Fri 10-4.30, Sat &
Sun 9-4.30; www.rhs.org.uk**

p. 160 Brooklands Museum **Open all year, Sats, Suns and BH
Mon; www.brooklandsmuseum.com**

p. 163 Great Cockrow Railway **May-Oct Sundays 2-5; www.
cockrow.co.uk**

p. 170 Thorney Country Park **Open access all year, no
visitor centre; www.buckscc.gov.uk**

p. 177 Runnymede **Open reasonable times daily all year;** **www.nationaltrust.org.uk**

p. 177 Air Forces Memorial **Summer Mon-Fri 9-6, weekends and BH Mon 10-6; closes at 4 in the winter**

p. 177 Royal Holloway College **Check website for event details at www.rhul.ac.uk or telephone on 01784 434455**

p. 188 St. Laurence's, Upton **Services on 1st Sun at 8 and 11, 2nd-5th Sun 11 only. Tues 2.30 toddlers, Thurs 10 Holy Communion**

p. 191 Pinewood Studios **Only open for special events; visit www.pinewoodshepperton.com for details or telephone 01753 656844**

p. 206 Colne Valley Park Visitors' Centre, Denham **Telephone 01895 833375 for details; www.colnevalleypark.org.uk**

p. 206 Milton's Cottage **Mar-Oct daily except Mon (but including BH Mons) 10-1, 2-6; www.miltonscottage.org**

p. 209 Basing House **Apr-Sep, Wed-Sun 2-6; www.hants.gov.uk**

p. 210 Jordans **Meetings Sun 10.30; 01494 874146**

p. 210 Moor Park **Tours Apr-Sep, one Thurs a month or groups by prior arrangement, tel 01923 773146**

p. 233 Mosquito Aircraft Museum **Mar-Oct, Tues, Thurs & Sat 2-5.30, Sun & BH Mon 10.30-5.30; www.dehavillandmuseum; co.uk**

p. 248 Capel Manor Gardens **Mar-end Oct, daily 10-4.30, garden**

closes 6; Nov-Feb weekends only, 10-4.30, garden closes 6;
www.capelmanorcollege.co.uk

p. 248 Rye House **Easter-end Sep, weekends & BH Mon 11-5;**
www.leevalleypark.org.uk

p. 254 Lea Valley Park Visitors' Centre **Mon-Fri 1-4, weekends**
10-5; tel 01992 702200; www.leevalleypark.org.uk

p. 261 Royal Gunpowder Mills **End Apr-end Sep, weekends & BH**
Mon 11-3.30 (last visit; closes 5); www.royalgunpowdermills.com

p. 266 Lakeside Shopping Centre **Mon-Fri 10-10, Sats 9-7.30, Sun**
11-5, BH Mon 10-6; www.lakeside.com

p. 273 Copped Hall **Guided walks 3rd Sun each month 10.45.**
For open days during the year and groups call 020 7267 1679

p. 274 Queen's Standing **Wed-Sun 1-4; www.cityoflondon.gov.uk**

p. 280 Hill Hall **Apr-end Sep, pre-booked tours on Wed only call**
01223 582 700; www.english-heritage.org.uk

p. 285 Nuclear Bunker **Daily Mar to Oct, Thur-Sun only Nov to**
Feb, 10-4; www.secretnuclearbunker.co.uk

p. 273 Belhus **8-dusk;** www.essexcc.gov.uk

IN 1957 THE AUTHOR BEGAN his National Service. He was told that a classics degree was of little use in the army and that he would be trained as a surveyor. Three months later he left for Cyprus as a Greek interpreter. There, sitting idly outside his tent he noticed three signallers enter right pushing three batteries in a wheelbarrow. They exited left. A furious Turk erupted then onto the scene. The CO was called and wanted to know what the fuss was about. The author suggested it might be the loss of the wheelbarrow. Thus was the author credited with speaking Turkish, and his miserable efforts in that direction led to him eventually working in a Turkish school, teaching English with, he thought, little success.

About the author

Back in London he followed his father into a West End firm dealing in antiquities. During this period he entered a large grill restaurant in Leicester Square to be greeted by 'Hullo, Sir' from the entire Turkish staff. Success of a sort.

After seven years in antiquities it became evident that the treasure house of Victorian collecting had been emptied and there was little left to deal in. Interested in his own young children, the author took a course in primary teaching, where he worked for twelve years. Tempted back to the adult world by his wife's success in the fashion business, he joined her, but was frustrated by the recession of 1989-90. It was then that the romance of the open road beckoned and, en route to Gatwick or Heathrow, he began his regular circumnavigations of the M25.

Roy can be found most mornings between 9.30 and 11 at the Costa Coffee in Bluewater.

THIS BOOK WOULD HAVE BEEN much the poorer without the archive and aerial photography kindly provided by the Kent Messenger, Philip Lane, Realistic and Simmons Aerofilms. Thanks also to the National Trust, and to John Turnbull for his view of the QE2 bridge at night.

Acknowledgements

All round the motorway the librarians of the public libraries have been exceptionally helpful, rooting out material from their local studies sections with encouragement rather than complaint. I must mention the librarians of Gravesend, Dartford, Sevenoaks, Reigate, Chertsey, Slough, Rickmansworth, Watford, Enfield, Brentwood and Thurrock. Dozens of individuals freely gave of their time to answer questions and only two, for security reasons, refused permission to photograph.

I went to the publishers, Pallas Athene, following the success of *A272: An Ode to a Road*. I have never regretted it; without the aid of Alexander Fyjis-Walker this book would have remained a scribble.   **RP**

The publisher would like to thank Mary Spence and Alan Smith at Global Mapping for their strong interest in the project; Chris Marshall of www.cbrd.com for his enthusiasm in preparing the junction diagram; and Demi Ross and Svetlana at Olympic for their tireless scanning of the pictures. Chris Mawson at Aerofilms, Sylvia Keith at Copped Hall, Lyn Chevalier of W. S. Atkins, Julia Kenny at Pinewood, Sue Thompson at the RHS and Philippa at Edifice Photo were all very helpful in finding photographs.

Further thanks to John H. Sutton for pointing the way for design, to Carol Farley for all her advice and cheer, and as always to Barbara Fyjis-Walker for proof-reading, and to James Sutton for wise encouragement. Above all thanks to Roy for his endless ability to take every kind of trouble, his tireless sense of amusement and his long-tried patience.   **AFW**

ALL PICTURES BY ROY PHIPPEN except: pp. 23, 45, 60, 62, 63, 95, 131, 144, 160, 203, 302 Philip Lane; p. 188 courtesy The Orpheus Trust; pp. 30-31 courtesy of John Turnbull; pp. 8-9, 35, 36-7, 38, 311 courtesy of the Kent Messenger; p. 53 courtesy of The Crossness Engines Trust, © Jerry Young; pp. 271 & 272 courtesy of Sylvia Keith, ARPS, APAGB, author of the book *Nine Centuries of People at Copped Hall*; p. 200 Marcus Taylor, Leonard and Marcus Taylor Ltd.; pp. 39, 50, 97, 1667, 198, 299 Simmons Aerofilms; p. 175 courtesy of W. S. Atkins plc; p. 191 courtesy of Pinewood Shepperton plc; p. 159 courtesy of Royal Horticultural Society; p. 189 courtesy of Andrew Taylor; p. 208 Edifice/Gillian Darley; pp. 201, 262-3 Realistic Chorley Handford; pp. 27, 140-141 courtesy of National Trust Regional Office; pp.156-7 courtesy of the Painshill Trust; p. 279 courtesy F. P. D. Savills; p. 184 © Museum of London; p. 276-277 Corporation of London; pp. 85, 125, 165 by J. H. Sutton, courtesy of the author; pp. 20, 25, courtesy Department of Transport; pp. 16, 100-1, 133, 136, 139, 152, 192, 210, 213, 238, 242, 248, 258-9 publisher's collection.

Prints of pictures used in this book may be obtained from the publisher. Write to Pallas Athene at 42 Spencer Rise, London NW5 1AP, or email info@pallasathene.co.uk

The toll plaza in earlier times

Entries in *italic*
refer to illustrations
or to captions

Index

A21 91, 93, 102
A22 90, 115
A30 170
A225 55
A25 89, 124
A282 see Dartford
  Crossing 34
Abbott, Richard and
  Doreen 110, 112
Abbotts Langley 197,
  198, 216, 218
Abercrombie Report
  20
Abernon, Sir John d'
  152, *152*
Abridge 281, *282*
Adrian IV, Pope 218
ague 300
Air Forces Memorial
  177, 307
Al Fayed, Mohammed
  115f
All Saints Pastoral
  Centre 222, *222*
Altman, Robert 236
Amersham 197
Anne of Cleves 119
Anne, Princess 272
Armada 293

'arterial' roads 19
Arun Canal 161
Asda 296
Ashstead 143, 145, 150
Ashstead Common
  150
Ashstead House 150
Aveley 300
Aylesbury 212
B2500 64
Babtie 41
Badgers Mount 85
Banstead 137
Barking 251
Barrett, John 300
Barrow Green Court
  116
Basing House 308
Batchworth Lock 206
beautiful bridge 59,
  60, 85
Becket 257
Beckton 53
Beckton Alps 53
Belhus 300f, *301*, 309
Bell Common Tunnel
  262, 265, 269
Bell Weir 179
Belvedere 53
Bentham, Jeremy 116
Betjeman, Sir John
  190
Biggin Hill 79, 105
Birch Hall 278
Black Death 216
Blackwall Tunnel 34
Bletchingley 82, 90, *90*,
  113, 114, 119, 121ff,
  122
Bligh, Captain 73
Blue Circle 43

Bluewater 55, 64, 65,
  65, *66*, 305
Botany Bay 228
Brands Hatch 72, *72*,
  305
Brasted 105
Breakspear, Nicholas
  218
Brentford 178, 205
Brentwood 289
bridges, girder 131,
  131
Brooklands 159, *161*
Brooklands Motor
  Museum 160, 307
Brookmans Park 237
Brown, Capability
  212, 301
Bruges 171
Buckingham Palace
  119, *121*
Buckland 135
Bulphan Fens 297
bunker see Secret
  Nuclear Bunker
Burghley, William
  Cecil, Lord 238,
  239
Burnham Beeches
  151, 191, *192*
Byng, General 235
Byng, Robert 236
Caesar, Julius 219
Calvert, Edward 81
Canary Wharf *3*, 204,
  251
canoeing 281
Capel Manor College
  247, *247*, 308
Capel, Sir Arthur 214,
  215

Capel, Sir William 247
Cassiobury 214, 216, 219
Cassivellaunus 219
Catherine Bourne 227
Chalfont St Giles 206
chalk 26f, 95, 111, 129, 130
Channel Tunnel Rail Link 48, *48*
Charles I 239
Charles II 104, *136*, 177, 181, 210, 211, 215, 248
Charterville 208
Chartist movement 206
Chartwell 104, 305
Chatley Heath Semaphore Tower *154*, 155, 306
Chertsey 165
Chertsey Abbey 83, 176
Chess, River 27, 178, 204, 209
Chevening 28, 60, 91, 98, *100*
Chigwell 117
Chingford 252
Chipstead 91
Churchill, Winston 104, *104*
Civil and Marine 46
Clacket Services 68, *86*, 98, 107, *107*, 110, 296
Clackett's Lane 107
Clayton, Sir Robert 112ff, *114*, 120, 292
coach road 231

Cobbett, William 181, 182
Cobelfreight 42, *45*
Cockcrow Hill 163f
Cofiroute 41
Colman, Jeremiah 135
Colnbrook 180
Colne, River 27, 178, 187, 199, 204, 209, 242
Colne Valley 170, 204
Colne Valley Park 169, 307
Colthurst, Edward 242, 243
Copped Hall 265, 270, *271*, 278, 309
Corporation of the City of London 22, 151, 274
Coventry, Lord 234, 235
Cowans, General Sir John 190
cricket 82
cricket pitch (Epping Foresters) *262*, 269
Cromwell, Oliver 137, 214, 234, 240, 248
Cromwell, Oliver (18th century) 240
Crossness sewage works 53, *53*, 305
Croydon Airport 185
Cuffley 249
Cuttes, Sir John 232
cyclists 34, *35*
d'Abernon family 152, *152*
Darenth interchange J2 64

Darenth Valley 59, 62, 73ff, *80*, 130, 169, 187
Darenth, River 27, 59, 68, *68*
Dartford 53, 62, 68, 174
Dartford River Crossing 30, 34ff, *35, 36, 38, 39, 40, 44*, 61, 147, 201, 227, 266, 303
de Mandeville family 234
deer parks 76f, 120, 289
Denham 206
Denmark, Christian IV, king of 239
Derby, The 138
Dodderidge, Sir John 177
Domesday Book 233
Dorking 130, 145
Duke of Northumberland's River 27, 187
Eagle Heights 79f, *79*, 305, view from *80*
Earl Stanhope, 7th 102
East Molesey 143
Eddie Stobart 295
Edith of the Swan Neck 257
Edward I 256
Edward III 216
Edward VI 271
Egham 176
Eleanor of Castile 216, 254, *254*, 256

Elizabeth I 119, 180, 234, 238, 274, *274*
Enfield 82, 228, 243
Enfield Chase 228, 233, 234
Epping Forest 137, 151, 228, 257, 265, 265, 269, 273, *275*, 276
Epsom 138
Essex, Arthur Capel, Earl of 214, 215
Essex, Earls of (Capel) 214
Essex, Earls of (Mandeville) 234
Evelyn, John 112, 138, 211, 214, 215, 216, 234
Eynsford *74, 76*
Fairey's Aerodrome 184
Farningham 73, *73*
Fire and Iron Gallery 151, *151*, 306
Ford Motor Company 266, 291
forests 137, 269, 273
Foster, Sir Robert 177
Fox, Charles James 164
Franks Farm 294
Frith, John 105
Fuller's *Worthies* 218, 260
Gade Valley Viaduct 147, *194*, 197, 200, *201*
Gade, River 27, 178, 197, 204, 209
gantries 146, *151*

Gatton 129, 135; Town Hall *134*, 135
Gatwick Airport 125
Gault clay 26, *86*, 96, *96*
geology 26f
George I 99, 102
Gibraltar 236
Globe Theatre 151
Godstone 112, 118
Godstone Police Centre 117, *117*
Godstone Vineyard 116, 306
Gosford Park 236
Grand Surrey Iron Railway 133
Grand Union Canal 27, 170, 197, 204f, 205
Gravelly Hill 124, 306
Gravesend 42
Grays Thurrock 52
Great Cockrow Railway 163f, *163*, 307
Great Fosters 177
Great North Road 231
Green Belt 22
greensand 95
Greenwich 243
Greenwich meridian 112, 257
Gresham family 105ff
Gresham, Sir John 105
Gresham, Sir Thomas 106
Groves 291
Guildford 161
gunpowder 260

Hainault 273
Hamilton, Hon. Charles 158
Hampton 179, 182
Hampton Court 82, 84, 143, 187
Hansard 105
Harefield 197
Hargreaves, Alice 105
Harold, King 257
Hart family 79
Hart-Dyke family 79
Hastings 102
Hatfield House 239, 271
Havering atte Bower 265
Hawkers 184
Headley Court 139
Heathrow 181, 182, 184ff, *184*
Heneage, Thomas 272
Henry II 257
Henry III 120
Henry VII 187
Henry VIII 78, 84, 119, 135, 187, 214, 218, 232, 257, 274, 300
Heronsgate 206f, *208*
Herschel, Sir William 188, *189*
Hertford 243, 251, 256
Heston 117, 184
Hill Hall 265, 279, *279*, 309
Hilliard, Nicholas 180
Hoddesdon 248
Holloway, Sir Thomas 177
Holmesdale Tunnel 228, *229*, 230, 269

Honeylands 247
Horton Kirby 68
Hotels 49
Hounslow Heath 181
Howard family 119, 150
Huygens, Sir Constantine 237
Hythe End 178
igloo *62, 69, 69*
ironworks 107
Isfahan 64
Isleworth 186, 187
J. F. Kennedy memorial 177
Jacobs, Michael 81
James I 78, 177, 234, 238, *238*, 239, 246
James II 237, 248
Jeffries, Judge 211
Jonson, Ben 239
Jordans 209, 308
Keeler, Christine 280
Kelvedon Hatch 265, 285
Kemps Farm 267, 294
Kempton Park 190
Kilns 111, *111*
King's Cut 187
Kings Langley 82, 197, 216, 218
Kingston, Mr. & Mrs. 285, 288
Kingswood the Forest 135
Kip, Johannes *100*
Kuhne, Eric 64
Lakeside Shopping Centre 47, *49, 50, 266*, 267, 308
Larbourne Pond 170

Le Crossing 41
Lea, River 27, *178*, 204, 229, 242, 251, 253, *253*, 254, 260, 261, 281
Lea Navigation 27, 205, 229, *250*, 251, 254
Lea Valley Park 169, 254
Leatherhead 143, 145, 150
Leatherhead by-pass *144*, 145
Lend Lease 64
Leoni, Giacomo 212
Leukenor, Sir Roger 233
Leverhulme, Lord 212
Leveson Gower family 107
Lewes 116
Liddell, Alice 105
Limpsfield 90
London Bridge 132, 178
London clay 267
London Colney 223
London Ring Main 179
Longford 180
Longford, River 187
Longside Lake 177
lorries 131, 295, *296*
Lullingstone Roman villa 76, *76*, 79, 305
Lullingstone Castle 29, 76ff, *77*, 305
Lutyens, Sir Edwin 171, *171, 172*
M1 199, *202*, 203
M3 *166*

M4 174, *175*
M23 97, 129
M26 91, 93
Macaulay, Thomas 28, 113, 248, 284
Maggot, Sir Richard 138
Magna Carta 177, monument 177, *177*
Man with the Star 102
Manson, W. J. 135
Mar Dyke *cover*, 27, 267, 270, 297, *297*, *298*, 300,
Marden 112
Mary I, Queen 271
Medway, River 152
Merstham 129, 132, 133
Meux, Lady 241
Meux, Sir Henry 240
Middleton, Sir Thomas 243
Miller, Bert 278
Milton's Cottage 206, 307
Minorca 99, 236
Misbourne, River 27, 178, 197, 199, 200, *200*
Mogador 138
Mole, River 27, 143, 150, 151, 152, 155
Monmouth, James Fitzroy, Duke of 210f, 215, 248
Moor Park 210ff, *210*, *213*, 308
Moor Park (nr. Farnham) 212
Mordaunt family 113

Mordaunt, Lord
Henry 120
Morison, Sir Richard
214
Morton, H.V. 185
Mosquito Aircraft
Museum 232, *232*,
308
motorways 21
muckshift 63, *63*
Napsbury 199
National Trust 104,
162
New Haw Viaduct
144, 147, 162, *162*,
201
New River 27, 229,
242ff, *243, 244*, 253,
254
Nonsuch 136, *136*
Norbert Dentresangle
295
Norman Conquest
234
North Downs 26
North Weald 280
Northfleet 42
Nuclear Bunker *see*
Secret Nuclear
Bunker
O'Connor, Feargus
206, 207, 209
O'Connorville 207
oast house 64
Oatlands 83, 137
Oatlands Palace 161
Ockendon 267, *293*
Ockendon Hall 291
Ockendons 297
Ockham Common
153

Old Palace House 240
Ordnance Survey 182
Orpheus Trust 118,
118, 306
Osterley Park 106
Otford 82f, *83*, 119,
137
Ouse, River 152
Ovaltine Egg Farm
198, 218
Ovaltine Factory 218f,
220
Oxford Canal 205
Oxted 93
Painshill 155f, *156*, 306
Palmer, Samuel 80f,
81
Park Gate House 59
Parkwood Hall 59, 68
Peche family 79
Peche, Sir John 78
Penn, William 209
Pepys, Samuel 104,
138
Perry Oaks Works 186
Petriches 247
Pevsner, Sir Nikolaus
270, 279
Pilgrim's Way 99
Pinewood Studios
191, *191*, 307
Pitt, William the
Younger 104
Pitt, Lucy 99
police 117, *117, 231,
233*
pollarded trees 78
Poplars 266, 285, *286,
288*
Portsmouth 155, 161,
162

Potters Bar 228, 233,
234, 237, 249, 289
power station 33, 49,
266
Poyle 180
Prescott, George 240
Prince of Wales 102
Prince's Covert 135
private finance initia-
tive 40
Procter and Gamble
47, *47*
Public Enquiries 23f,
63, 91, 130, 186
Purfleet 52
Purfleet Hotel 267
Pyrford Lock 159
Quakers 209
quarries 43, *90*, 111,
116
Quebec House 104,
305
Queen Elizabeth II
bridge 33, 37, *38, 39*,
45 *also see* Dartford
Crossing
Queen's Cut 187
Queen's Standing 274,
275, 309
RAF 280 *also see*
Biggin Hill *and* Air
Forces Memorial
railway 48, *48*, 143,
147, *148, 163*, 163,
197, 199f, *200*
Ranger's House,
Blackheath 150
Redwell Wood Farm
227
Reform Bill 135
Reigate 130, 133, 227

Reigate Golf Club 129, 133
Reigate Hill *126*, 129, 133, 199
Renewable Energy Systems 219
reservoirs 178f
Richard Rumbold 248
Richmond, George 81
Rickmansworth 204, 206, 209
ring roads 17
Ringway 41
Robertson, Archibald 178, 188
Robinson, Lt William Leefe 249
Roding, River 27, 264, 281
Roman road 28, 107, 116, 242, 286
Roy, General 181f, *183, 304*
Royal Aeronautical Society 184
Royal Alexandra and Albert School 135
Royal Gunpowder Mills 261, 308
Royal Holloway College 177, 307
Royal Horticultural Society 158f, *159*, 306
Royal Powder Magazines 52
Runnymede 174, 176, 177, *177, 179*, 307
Russell, Lord 215
Rye House 210, 248, *248*, 308

Rye House Plot 210, 248f
Sainsbury's 296
Salisbury Hall 227, 232
Saltonstall, Sir Richard 292f, *292*
saltpetre 79, 260
Savacentre 223
Saxon burial ground 95, *95*
Secret Nuclear Bunker 285, *285*, 309
Sevenoaks 62, 85, 89, 91
sewage 53, 186, 305
Shenley 199, 227, 233
Shoreham 80f, *81*
Sitwell, Sacheverell 114
Slough 188ff, *189*, 307
Smith family 280
Smith, Sir Thomas 279
Society of All Saints Sisters of the Poor 223
Somers, Lord John 236
South Mimms *224*, 227, 230, 231, 233, 234, 289
South Park Hotel 235
speed limits 146
Squerryes 98, 103f, *103*, 305
St Albans 64, 216, 219
St Anne's Hill *164*, 174
Stafford family 119

Staines 171, 204
Stanhope family 150
Stanhope, Earl (General James Stanhope) 28, 98, 120
Stanhope, Lady Hester 104
Stansted 36
Stapleford Airport 265, 280
Star Hill 102
Stilgoe, Richard 118
Stoke d'Abernon 143, 152, *152*
Stoke D'Abernon school 153
Straw, Jack 102
Sutton 136
Sutton Place 265
Suttons 281f, *284*
Swanley 59
Swanley Maintenance Compound 69, *70*
Swanley roundabout J3 61, *62*
TASIS 176
Tatling End 197
Taylor, Andrew *189*
Telford, Thomas 231
Temple Bar 241, *241*
Temple, Sir William 212
Tennyson, Alfred, Lord 257
Tesco 296
Thames, River 27, 143, 161, 162, 169, 178, *179*, 180, 187, 204, 205, 228, 243, 251, 281 *also see*

Dartford River Crossing
Thames Europort 43
Thatcher, Margaret 230
Theobalds 78, 237, 238, 239, 240, 242, 246
Theydon Bois 265, 278
Thorney Country Park 170, 307
Thorney Deep 170
Thorpe 176
Titsey 89, 98, 105f, *106*, 306
Titsey South Lodge *108*, 110
traffic jam *16*
Truck World 296
trucks *see* lorries
Turner's Hill 151
ugly bridge 147, *148*, 165
Upton, St Laurence's Church *189*, 307
Uxbridge 170
Van den Berg 46
Van Omeren 43, 47
Verderers 137
Victoria, Queen 274, *276*
Victoria and Albert Museum 256

Viner, Mr. & Mrs. 102
vineyard 90, 116, 306
Voltaire 236
waggons 132f, *133*, 252, 254
Waltham Abbey 254, 257, *257*, *258*, *260*, 271, 273
Waltham Cross 112, 254, *254*
Waltham, Abbot of 252
Wandsworth 133
Warde family 103
Warde, Sir John 104
Wareham, Archbishop William 83
Warley 291
Warwick 205
water tower *124*, 125
Watford 20, 21, 24, 198, 204, 212
Watling Street 64, 219
Weald 89, 289
Weald Hall 289, *290*
Welwyn 117
West Molesey 143
Westerham 68, 98, 103f
Westerham Green 104, *104*
Westminster Abbey 132

Wey Navigation Canal 27, *27*, 144, 147, 160, 205
Wey, River 27, *140*, 159
Weybridge 137
Whipsnade Zoo 278
Whitbread, Josiah 52
Wiggley Bush Lane 289
Willi Betz 295
William I 152
William III 28, 237
Windsor Castle 132
Wisley *see* Royal Horticultural Society
Woldingham School 115
Wolfe, General 104
Wolsey, Cardinal Thomas 84, 210
Woolwich 53, 260
Woolwich Free Ferry 34
Worth Forest 151
Wraysbury, River 27, 178, 187
Wren, Sir Christopher 241
Wrotham Park 93, 235, 236, *236*, 237

M25: Travelling Clockwise
© Roy Phippen 2005
The moral right of the author
has been asserted

Editor: Alexander Fyjis-Walker

Maps by Mary Spence at Global Mapping.
Map on inner flyleaf © XYZ Maps 2005
All other maps except p. 24
© Crown copyright 2005. All rights reserved.
Licence number 100038939/400002435
Diagrams in back flyleaves and on p. 24
by Chris Marshall for Pallas Athene,
© Pallas Athene 2005.
For all things motorwayan,
visit Chris's website www.cbrd.co.uk

Scanning by Olympic Press, London

First published 2005
by Pallas Athene (Publishers) Ltd
42 Spencer Rise, London NW5 1AP

If you would like further information about
Pallas Athene publications,
please write to the address above,
or visit our website:

www.pallasathene.co.uk

ISBN 1-873429-90-8

Printed in China

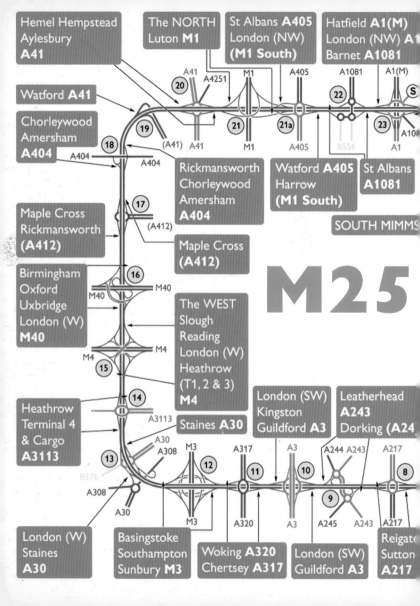